DREAMWORKS
ANIMATION SKG

For my very own Snack Pack of Trolls: Katie, Allison, Kyle, Kiera, and Sophie —*J.S.*

The Art of DreamWorks Trolls • ISBN: 9781785653025

Published by Titan Books
A division of Titan Publishing Group Ltd.
144 Southwark St., London, SE1 0UP

First edition: September 2016 • 10 9 8 7 6 5 4 3 2 1

To receive advance information, news, competitions, and exclusive offers online, please sign up for the Titan newsletter on our website: www.titanbooks.com

Did you enjoy this book? We love to hear from our readers. Please e-mail us at:readerfeedback@titanemail.com or write to Reader Feedback at the above address.

A CIP catalogue record for this title is available from the British Library.

Printed and bound in China.

Page 1: Moon Boy • Priscilla Wong; *Right*: Purple Dusk • Timothy Lamb; *Below*: Troll Village Leaf • Avner Geller; *Following pages*: Troll Forest Texture and Color • Nicholas Henderson; *Pages 6–7:* Troll Forest • Ken Pak; *Page 7, clockwise from top left:* Smidge's Birthday Invitation • Clio Chiang; Troll Village Invitations • Ken Pak; Cake Topper • Avner Geller; Lollipop • Avner Geller; Invitation • Avner Geller

The Art of

DreamWorks

Trolls

Foreword by Anna Kendrick

Written by Jerry Schmitz

Book design by Iain R. Morris & Barbara Genetin

TITAN BOOKS

London

Contents

Poppyz Friendz
Smidge's B-day
Pizza Party
Branch
You're Invited

Foreword

When I met with Mike Mitchell and Walt Dohrn two years ago and they asked me to voice the role of Princess Poppy, I was thrilled but I felt obligated to make sure that they had the right girl. I hardly felt like the person to play the happiest Troll in all the land; sugary sweet isn't really my forte. I warned them that I might lead Poppy down a feistier path. I think I used the term "spark plug," but that was code for "a little bit crazy."

Each time I stepped into the recording booth and was greeted by a picture of Poppy's smiling face, I couldn't wait to add some fire and determination to her little character. That said, I usually ruined the first five minutes of each session by talking in my "adorable voice." I couldn't help it! She's so cute! But Mike and Walt encouraged me to make this tiny pink creature feel real and complicated. Poppy might not look like Shrek, but she's got layers.

After many months of recording, I was feeling greedy and asked if I could see some footage and learn a little bit more about the artwork. The DreamWorks department heads put together a presentation for me that made me realize what a tiny corner of the *Trolls* universe I had seen.

Down in my recording booth, I'd been testing the waters with little screwball tones and I was thrilled to find that the dream team at DreamWorks had captured that little firecracker inside Poppy with every minute expression. This is nothing new for them, of course—they've been filling their characters with humanity and complexity film after film.

What *was* new was the handmade, tactile style of animation they created for the magical world of *Trolls*. Taking inspiration from a variety of time periods and cultures, the animators were creating something completely unique for the *Trolls* universe. So much love, passion, and hard work was put into the execution of every frame. I continue to be blown away by the talent behind this film, and I hope you love learning about the artistry as much as I did.

Anna Kendrick

P.S. Mike Mitchell, Walt Dohrn, Gina Shay, and Jeffery Katzenberg: Thank you so much for letting me be a part of this film, it's been a dream—a joyous, feisty, psychedelic dream.

Above: Butterfly • Amélie Fléchais; *Opposite*: Poppy Final Character Render • DreamWorks Animation

Introduction

DreamWorks' *Trolls* reunites the directors and producers behind the studio's block-buster hit *Shrek Forever After*, with Director Mike Mitchell, Producer Gina Shay, and Co-Director Walt Dohrn leading the production. "I worked closely with Mike and Walt on *Shrek Forever After* and I knew that if I could lure them into the world of *Trolls*, they would make it brilliantly unexpected," says Shay.

"Spending so much time in the world of Ogres, we were bound to be led to their not-so-distant cousins from Scandinavian mythology—the Trolls," says Dohrn.

While conducting research for the film, the filmmakers delved into Troll lore, soon learning that Trolls come in various shapes and sizes—from monstrous giants that eat children to tiny creatures who grant wishes.

According to legend, Trolls have been lurking in caves and forests, inside logs and under bridges for centuries. Sometimes perceived as mischievous and canny, Trolls can also bring good luck to those who come in contact with them.

"As Walt and I dug further into the popularity of Trolls and traced them into modern times, some recurring themes began to emerge," says Mitchell. "Trolls have progressed from their menacing origins to become happy creatures. Their simplicity and imperfections have become more relatable, making people feel good."

That simple theme of "happiness" pervading modern troll lore is what eventually proved so compelling to the filmmakers. "We decided that it was time to start spreading happiness again," continues Mitchell.

To start their cinematic quest for happiness, the crew naturally turned to the modern craze that cemented Trolls' association with joy: the Troll dolls.

The Troll dolls have an origin story that is now legend in its own right. Nearly sixty years ago, Danish woodcutter and fisherman Thomas Dam did not have enough money to purchase a Christmas gift for his young daughter Lila. Relying on his skills as a craftsman, Dam carved a doll out of wood, letting his imagination guide him.

Young Lila soon became the envy of every child in her hometown of Gjøl, Denmark. Before he could say "Troll," Thomas Dam had himself a cottage industry. It wasn't long after Dam's initial Christmas gift to his daughter that he began making Troll dolls—known as "Dam Dolls"—for the locals.

With the formation of the Dam Things Company, Thomas Dam expanded his production output (switching from wood to plastic) and set up distribution. Following an international heyday in the 1960s—when they were second in popularity only to Barbie—Trolls have been a global phenomenon for decades.

In discussing the creative direction and tone of the film with the Dam Things Company, the filmmakers explained that they wanted to honor the essential characteristics of the original dolls while adding features that would make the characters in the film more distinguishable from one another. "We knew that by making them unique, it would broaden the depth of our story and world," explains Shay. "We also felt that we could enhance their visual uniqueness by flocking their skin and making them every color of the rainbow."

For Mitchell, the fact that the Troll dolls created by Dam did not really have a backstory proved liberating. "We had a blank slate from which we could craft our narrative," explains the director. "We could literally do anything and go anywhere with these characters!"

"We wanted to tell an old-fashioned fairy tale but with a subversive edge," adds Dohrn. "The Trolls, with all their quirkiness and irreverence, felt very 'fairy tale' to us and the story itself came together very naturally."

"Mike and Walt's crazy ideas started on a napkin, and, with the help of our writers, were crafted on Mike's llama, sheep,

Opposite, top: Troll Village Pod House Lineup • Avner Geller; *Opposite, bottom*: Troll Dolls • Photograph by Samantha Trauben; *Right*: Travel Concept • Amélie Fléchais; *Below*: Llamas photograph • Gina Shay

and chicken farm in Northern California," adds Shay. "It helped us on our fuzzy and psychedelic path."

For Production Designer Kendal Cronkhite-Shaindlin, the doll came first. "When I was thinking about characters, I knew we didn't want them to be human, but rather magical forest sprites," she explains. "I started to think they shouldn't have skin but something else, nonhuman."

In researching the project, Cronkhite-Shaindlin observed that one version of the Dam Troll Doll had felted and glitter skin with gem belly buttons. "We embraced this idea by adding a level of gummy-bear, saturated color translucency underneath, which was actually [Art Director/Character Designer] Timothy Lamb's idea, which made the Trolls feel like succulent plants." That design concept carried over into the look of the forest as well. Continues Cronkhite-Shaindlin, "Because these little characters were living in perfect harmony with the forest, we wanted the forest to have those same textures. We landed on felt and all things fiber for the forest. Felting techniques, knit, macramé, and stitching were used for plants, ground, rock, clouds, and dirt—and we used glitter for all the magical effects in the film. We researched fiber and

slow art from all across the planet and were so inspired by fiber artists reinventing the natural world from wool and fabrics. Then the question became, 'How can we possibly create this fuzzy world in CG?'"

As the story began to take shape, the filmmakers decided to center their tale on two Trolls: Poppy (Anna Kendrick), a very determined Troll who is passionate about her point of view; and Branch (Justin Timberlake), her polar opposite.

To make the dynamic between two headstrong characters work, Mitchell looked to *Romancing the Stone*—one of his favorite films—for inspiration. "We knew our story would be told from both Poppy and Branch's points of view," says Mitchell. "The dynamic between Kathleen Turner and Michael Douglas—that push-me-pull-you energy and the way they played off each other—is something we wanted to see with Poppy and Branch."

Many of the filmmakers grew up in the 1970s, when Trolls dolls were everywhere, which naturally led them to draw on the aesthetics of that era as they developed the look of the film. Working with these more contemporary references led the DreamWorks team to question what a fairy tale is. "We all remember the '70s for different reasons," notes Mitchell, "but to kids today, the '70s is somewhat of a fairy tale world—one with phones that have cords attached to them!"

Ultimately, *Trolls* is a film about the value of happiness, where it comes from, the lengths people will go to get it, and whether happiness and positive thinking are strong enough to overcome the negative elements in the world. "The fundamental emotional theme in the film is that happiness comes from within and can be an infectious and powerful force when it's spread," says Shay.

Above: Troll Swimming Hole • Timothy Lamb; *Opposite*: Poppy and Branch • Timothy Lamb

"Mike Mitchell fell in love with Timothy Lamb's quirky, almost underground comic–like take on these characters. They were exactly what he envisioned for the film."
– Kendal Cronkhite-Shaindlin, Production Designer

HAPPY

MEET THE TROLLS

Hair & Hugs

When Thomas Dam made his first Troll doll for his daughter in Denmark in the late 1950s, he carved it out of wood and used lamb's wool for the hair and wool felt for the clothing. Production Designer Kendal Cronkhite-Shaindlin took this origin to heart when she began to develop the characters for DreamWorks Animation's *Trolls*. "I couldn't get the idea of this handmade object made from natural materials out of my head," recalls Cronkhite-Shaindlin. "I also thought the Trolls should be bright and multicolored."

Continues Cronkhite-Shaindlin, "I was first brought onto the project when all that was established was the doll, Director Mike Mitchell, Co-Director Walt Dohrn, and Producer Gina Shay." Cronkhite-Shaindlin's first task was to help the filmmakers "break the character code" for the film. For her, the Troll doll is an institution. "I remember how odd looking they were, kind of 'ugly-cute,' like babies and little old people all rolled up into one design."

In approaching the design, the filmmakers kept two things in mind: "ugly-cute" and "hair," especially. "Believe it or not, the Trolls are actually half hair," says Cronkhite-Shaindlin. "Our characters are six inches tall, and three inches of that is hair!"

Looking again to the first Troll toy for inspiration, the crew noticed that there wasn't a single straight line in its design. "The doll is stubby, with curved, plumped shapes everywhere," explains Cronkhite-Shaindlin, "so that became part of our characters' and world's shape language."

The design team embraced the doll's horizontal oval head and big ears. In researching the iconic figures, they discovered that creator Dam had designed different ears for the female and male Trolls, which evolved during the decades following

his initial creation—a detail they incorporated into the film's character designs.

Another key characteristic of Dam's original Troll dolls was their trademark black eyes. "We tried to incorporate that look into our characters, but we soon discovered that the design was very animalistic and really hard to relate to emotionally," says Cronkhite-Shaindlin, "so we abandoned that look in favor of an iris and eye white for our characters."

To further develop the look of the Trolls, Cronkhite-Shaindlin first hired veteran character designer Craig Kellman. "Craig infuses his characters with such amazing

Previous pages: Happy Forest • Priscilla Wong; *Top*: Glitter Poppy Stylization • Timothy Lamb; *Above*: Snack Pack Lineup • Willie Real; *Opposite*: Troll Dolls • Photograph by Samantha Trauben

comedic flavor," praises Cronkhite-Shaindlin. "He created these charming, funny little forest Trolls that were almost manic in their exaggerated movement and expressiveness."

Kellman drew inspiration from Max Fleischer and other iconic animators to create Troll designs that appealed to the filmmakers. Explains Kellman, "I wanted to combine those superugly faces with a cartoon appeal, specifically inspired by the Bob Clampett Warner Bros. shorts of the 1940s."

Inspired by Kellman's initial designs, Art Director/Character Designer Timothy Lamb then set out to incorporate some of the preliminary Troll characters into his early concept pieces and reworked what the final characters looked like by incorporating a more contemporary, underground, comic design style. "Updating a beloved classic like the Troll doll can be a difficult task," admits Lamb. "On one hand, the goal was to celebrate the charm and oddities of the original doll and find a way to preserve some of those qualities. On the other hand, we wanted to contemporize the doll, adding humor and appeal to give it our unique perspective."

Lamb and the filmmakers spent a great deal of time analyzing the original doll to determine what would end up in the final character designs. "Obviously, the hair was our first priority," he says. "Some of our early discussions were all about customizing the hairstyles of our main characters in order to give them their own identities."

Knowing that the original doll was carved out of wood and had lamb's wool for hair, the design team wanted the characters' final looks to be almost tactile. "Our goal was to avoid realism in skin textures and to accentuate the miniature scale and the tangible qualities of a real toy," says Lamb. "We ended up with a character that had a translucent, gummy-bear-like interior flocked with felt on the outside—almost like a succulent plant."

When you look closely, you will see that the Trolls do not vary too much in form and design. As Lamb explains, the filmmakers "wanted color to play a big role in defining each of the Trolls and their personalities. Every Troll has a unique combination of hair and skin color." These various combinations help differentiate the Trolls and also contrast markedly with the much larger, scarier Bergens.

With all that said, let's meet the Trolls!

Above: Troll Tree • Timothy Lamb; *Left*: Hairstylists • Willie Real; *Opposite*: Poppy and Branch • Timothy Lamb

Scrapbooking

The filmmakers knew from the very beginning that the world of the Trolls had to not only look different but feel different as well. Early in the design process, Director Mike Mitchell and Co-Director Walt Dohrn had a unique challenge for the art department: set up each major plot point of the film with storybook pages that look as if they came from a felted scrapbook.

"I was brought in fairly early on with the scrapbook concept," recalls Visual Development Artist Priscilla Wong. "The scrapbook pages represent Poppy's hand in the narration, so we knew finding the right look would be crucial."

For Wong, one of the biggest challenges was telling the simplified version of the story in the scrapbook medium, which she describes as "inherently busy." Balancing textures within graphic shapes also required some finesse and became crucial to her process.

Borrowing elements from around the house and office—such as aluminum foil, crushed peppermint candy, sponges, and a promotional wig from *Madagascar 3* (she flattened and separated the strands with a hair iron)—Wong created her first iteration of a few scrapbook pages complete with Trolls, rainbow wigs, and Bergens (which she gave "sponge eyebrows").

"The whole process felt a bit like the 'Unconventional Materials Challenge' from *Project Runway*," Wong jokes, "but we [she and Production Designer Kendal Cronkhite-Shaindlin] were thrilled with the outcome."

However, when they presented the designs to Mitchell and Dohrn, the directors "felt that everything was too articulated, too mature," recalls Wong. "Since my nature is to execute things impeccably, the main critique of the early scrapbook pages was that they looked too perfect—almost like a beautifully executed stop-motion film without the kitschy humor that defines our story."

Following Mitchell and Dohrn's direction to make the designs look more amateur, Wong went back to the scrapbooking board and focused more on traditional scrapbooking techniques. Relying heavily on craft-store materials, she incorporated a number of borders and graphics that convey more of a natural, handmade Scandinavian look and feel.

It was important for Mitchell that the scrapbook pages reflect, Wong says, "the hand of the artist," noting that the "pages needed to look handmade and effortless." This drove her to work more crudely, with more feeling and less precision, and to adapt her creative process. "After establishing the look of the scrapbook, their [Mitchell and Dohrn's] direction forced me to think more like a filmmaker than an illustrator," recalls Wong. "I took into consideration the camera movements, staging, transitions, animation, and effects—which ultimately forced me, in a good way, to set up a minipipeline for myself."

For each page, Wong would deliver an animated GIF as a proof-of-concept. Once that was approved, she would then craft each page and photograph it. These photos were then animated by After Effects Artist Erik Tillmans using various After Effects techniques.

The result—which made use of 1,751 pieces of felt in 98 different colors and 220 different colors of paper—is fifteen handmade scrapbook pages that tell the story of the film.

Wong's favorite scrapbook page is the one that sets up "Poppy's Journey." "It's the perfect mix of colors and textures that represents the Trolls' world intruded on by the Bergens," says the artist.

Opposite: Scrapbook Artwork • Priscilla Wong, photographs by Samantha Trauben; *Right, top to bottom*: Scrapbook Set • Sebastien Piquet; Lighting Key • Peter Zaslav; Priscilla Wong; Threading• Photograph by Samantha Trauben; Priscilla Wong's Screens • Photographs by Samantha Trauben; Priscilla Wong Working • Photographs by Samantha Trauben

This page: Scrapbook Artwork • Priscilla Wong, photograph by Samantha Trauben;
Opposite: Troll Forest Fiber Art • Sayuri Sasaki Hemann, photograph by Samantha Trauben

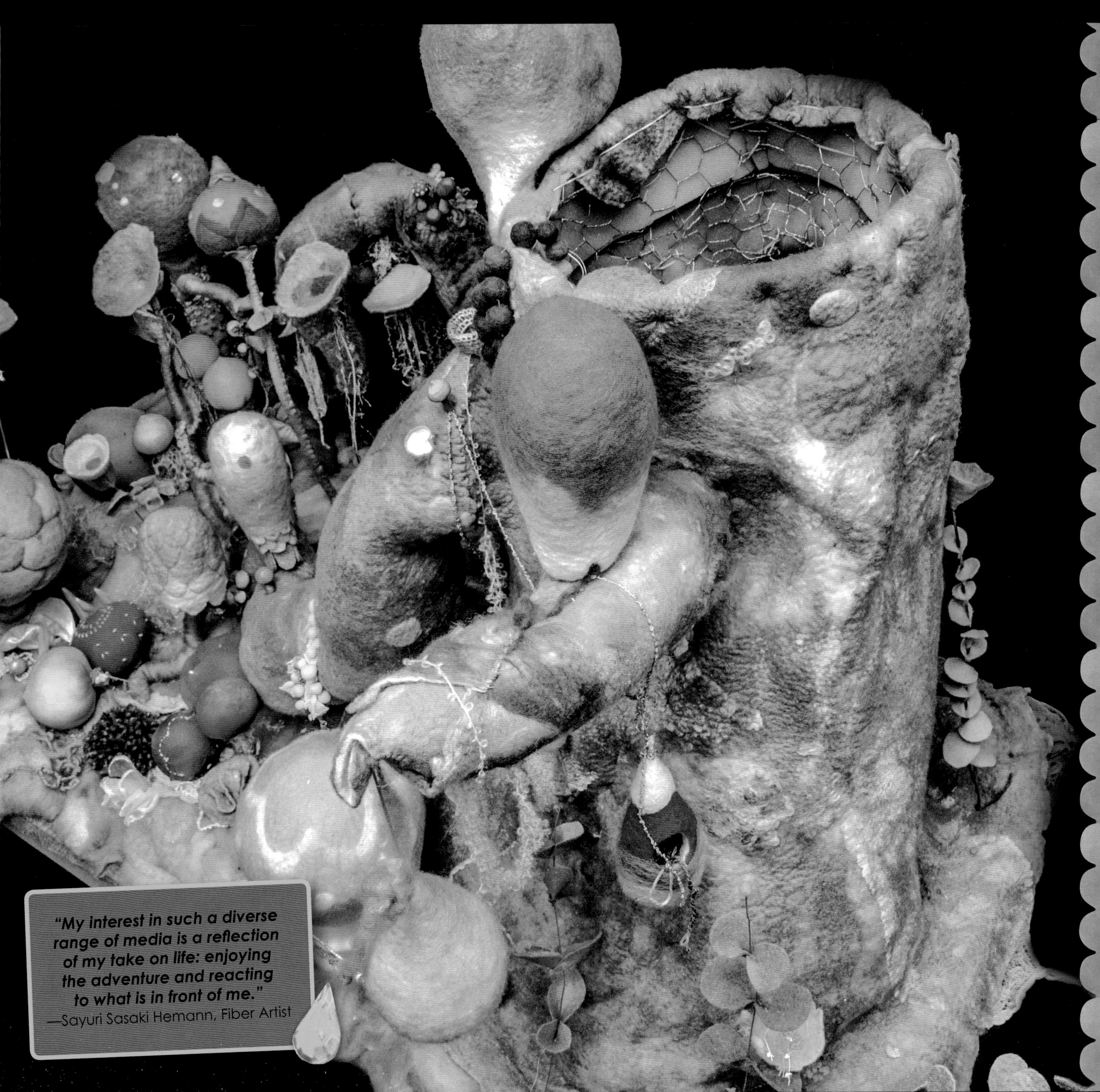
"My interest in such a diverse range of media is a reflection of my take on life: enjoying the adventure and reacting to what is in front of me."
—Sayuri Sasaki Hemann, Fiber Artist

Poppy

She's popular, she's perky, and, most of all, she's positive! "Poppy is the driving force of our story," explains Producer Gina Shay. "She embodies the qualities that all Trolls strive to achieve."

Princess of the Trolls and daughter of King Peppy, Poppy's duties are simple: keep everyone safe from the Bergens (who have not been seen in twenty years) and keep all the Trolls happy! Simple, right? Driven by her unyielding and infectious positivity, Poppy is cut from "an entirely new piece of princess cloth," according to Director Mike Mitchell.

Bringing to life the character of Poppy is Academy Award nominee Anna Kendrick. "She was always our first choice," says Mitchell. "Not only is she an incredible actress—she has an amazing voice. When she starts singing, it's as if she is performing a magic trick."

Adds Co-Director Walt Dohrn, "To top it all off, she [Kendrick] has this quirky edge to her personality that lends itself to Poppy's unique character texture."

Designing the look of Poppy started with understanding her core character traits. "The directors describe Poppy as energetic, smart, and eternally optimistic—a pure force of positivity almost to a fault," explains Art Director/Character Designer Timothy Lamb.

Lamb credits the initial design work of Character Designer Craig Kellman with inspiring his own early drawings of the character, in which Lamb translated Poppy's defining personality traits into the overall look of a Troll. "In our story, she's a princess, yet we didn't want her to look pretty or traditionally feminine," explains Lamb. "She's quirky and saccharine, imperfect and individualistic, so we wanted her design to have a sense of humor and break the archetype of a classic princess."

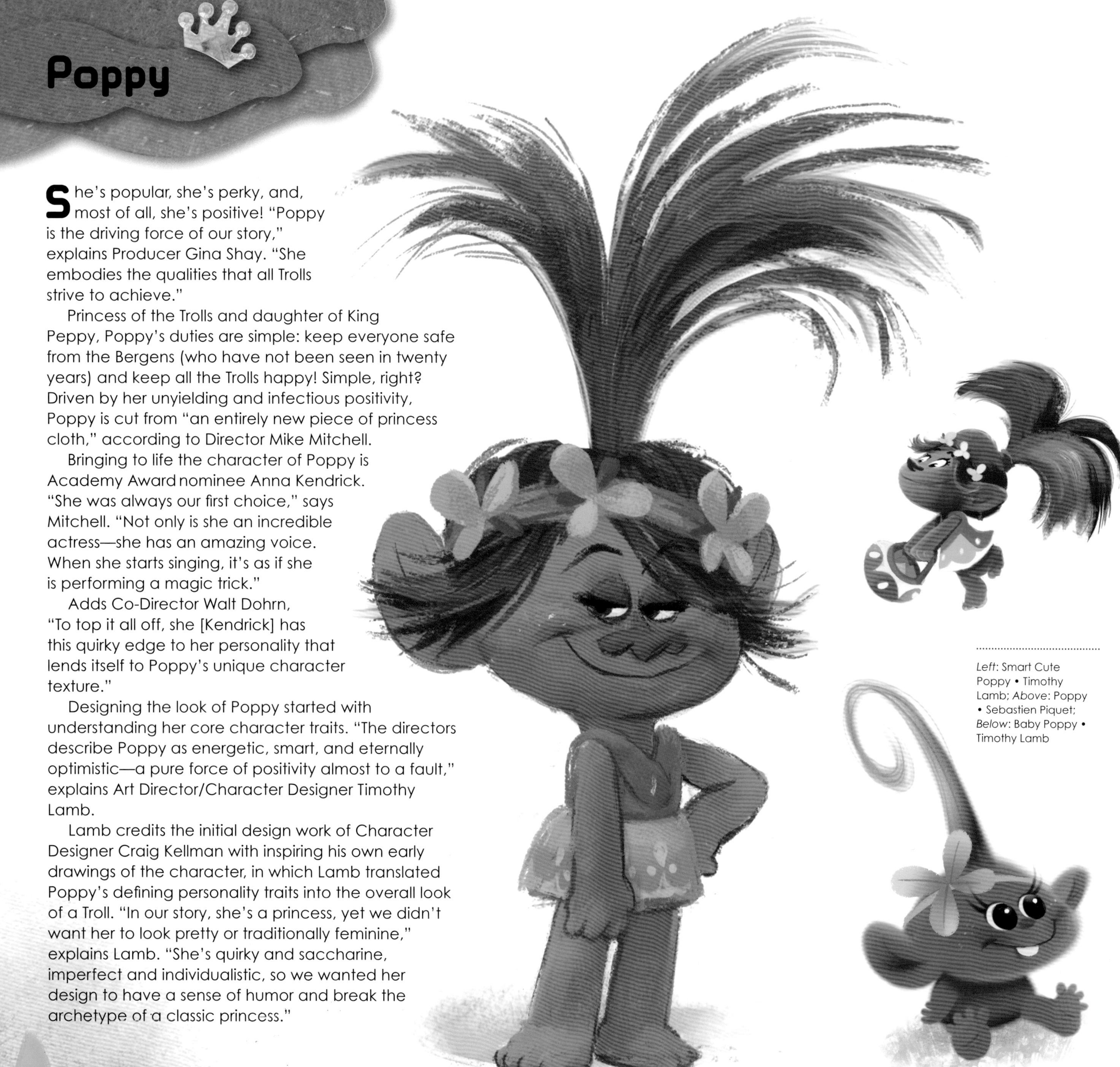

Left: Smart Cute Poppy • Timothy Lamb; *Above*: Poppy • Sebastien Piquet; *Below*: Baby Poppy • Timothy Lamb

Poppy's primary color, "Poppy Pink!," was chosen to communicate her positivity. Also, great attention was given to the style of her clothes and her hair ("It's all about the hair," says Producer Gina Shay) so they would telegraph Poppy's distinctive eccentricities. Some of these details were inspired by other fictional, nontraditional young women: "We started to think of her as a Pippi Longstocking or even a Punky Brewster type," adds Lamb. "I think that's where the ponytail came from . . . it's like an exploding volcano!"

This page: Poppy Character Studies • Craig Kellman

"Poppy's ponytail looks like an exploding volcano of pink hair."
—Timothy Lamb, Art Director/Character Designer

This page: Poppy Character Studies • Timothy Lamb; *Inset:* New Color Poppy • Craig Kellman

Above: Poppy Costumes • Priscilla Wong; *Below left*: Poppy Irritated • Timothy Lamb; *Inset*: Poppy Sad • Timothy Lamb; *Below right:* Poppy Confident • Timothy Lamb

Far left, top: Poppy • Priscilla Wong; *Far left, inset*: Poppy Web • Timothy Lamb; *Below*: Poppy Poses • Timothy Lamb; *Bottom*: Poppy Expressions • Timothy Lamb

Above and right: Poppy Clothes and Poses • Timothy Lamb; Far right: Poppy Final Character Render • DreamWorks Animation

"Happiness is inside all of us. Sometimes you just need someone to help you find it."
– Poppy

Branch

He's prickly, he pouts, and, most of all, he's pessimistic. In other words, Branch is the complete opposite of Poppy. He loathes Hug Time (he doesn't even wear a bracelet to keep himself on a proper Hug Time schedule).

Devoid of "color," Branch is convinced that the Bergens are destined to discover where the Trolls have been living peacefully these past couple of decades.

Ironically, the actor behind the voice of Branch is one of the most upbeat talents in the industry: multiple Grammy and Emmy Award winner Justin Timberlake. "What Justin brings to the table is nothing short of extraordinary," praises Producer Gina Shay.

When it came to designing Branch, the team had it relatively easy once Poppy's look was established: Branch is Poppy's opposite in every way possible. Branch hides and contains his enthusiasm; he is the pessimist and cynical foil to Poppy's perpetually upbeat character.

Recalls Art Director/Character Designer Timothy Lamb, "Branch's character was described to me as a survivalist, a kind of antisocial hermit living hidden away from the other Trolls. So it was easy to support that narrative by dressing him in handmade clothing patched together from leaves."

Because Trolls desaturate their colors when they are frightened or sad, Branch is in a permanent state of desaturation, making him blend into his environment and disappear. One with his surroundings, Branch is like a hunter-gatherer who carries a slingshot and a survival-kit backpack.

As with Poppy, the filmmakers emphasized his character traits through his design. This led to stark contrasts between Branch's and Poppy's predominant shapes and colors. Whereas Poppy is infused with saturated pinks and warm colors, Branch's palette is very gray with dark green and cool purple accents. His hair is also

Far left and top: Troll Snapshots • Timothy Lamb; *Left*: Branch Clothed • Timothy Lamb

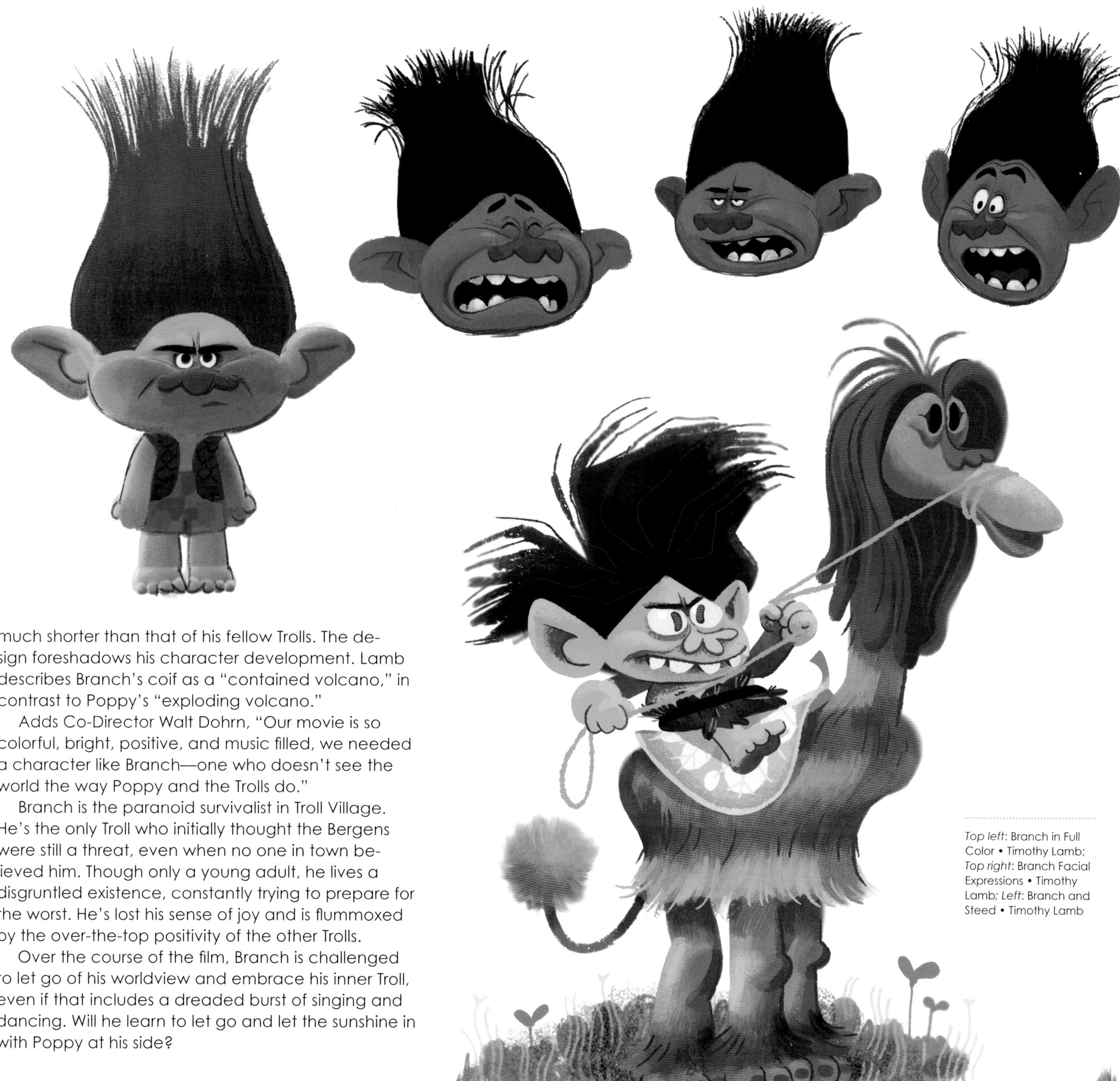

much shorter than that of his fellow Trolls. The design foreshadows his character development. Lamb describes Branch's coif as a "contained volcano," in contrast to Poppy's "exploding volcano."

Adds Co-Director Walt Dohrn, "Our movie is so colorful, bright, positive, and music filled, we needed a character like Branch—one who doesn't see the world the way Poppy and the Trolls do."

Branch is the paranoid survivalist in Troll Village. He's the only Troll who initially thought the Bergens were still a threat, even when no one in town believed him. Though only a young adult, he lives a disgruntled existence, constantly trying to prepare for the worst. He's lost his sense of joy and is flummoxed by the over-the-top positivity of the other Trolls.

Over the course of the film, Branch is challenged to let go of his worldview and embrace his inner Troll, even if that includes a dreaded burst of singing and dancing. Will he learn to let go and let the sunshine in with Poppy at his side?

Top left: Branch in Full Color • Timothy Lamb; *Top right*: Branch Facial Expressions • Timothy Lamb; *Left*: Branch and Steed • Timothy Lamb

"Careful consideration was taken in choosing the colors for Poppy and Branch and for the rest of the Trolls. We knew saturation and a wide range of color diversity was the best way to represent these happy little creatures."
—Timothy Lamb,
Art Director/Character Designer

This page: Branch Character Studies • Craig Kellman

Clockwise from top left: Branch Foraging • Avner Geller; Branch Expression • Craig Kellman; Branch Clothed • Timothy Lamb; Branch Foraging • Avner Geller; Branch Clothed • Timothy Lamb; Branch Backpacks • Avner Geller

Opposite, far left: Branch Final Character Render • DreamWorks Animation; *Opposite, top right*: Branch Character Studies • Craig Kellman; *Opposite, middle left*: Branch Sketch • Craig Kellman; *Opposite, middle right*: Branch's True Colors • Timothy Lamb; *Opposite, bottom right*: Branch in Color • Craig Kellman; *This page*: Branch and Poppy Final Character Renders • DreamWorks Animation

Biggie & Dinkles

Underneath Biggie's imposing exterior lies a cuddly softie. "He's basically a cat lady," says Co-Director Walt Dohrn.

Biggie is the biggest member of the Snack Pack *(see sidebar, opposite)* with the biggest heart. Touching moments, sunsets, and, of course, Poppy's positivity can turn him into a puddle of tears. In early stages of development, the character's name was actually "Big Guy, Easy Cry."

Biggie's pride and joy is his pet worm, Mr. Dinkles. He is quite the photographer, and his favorite pastime is to dress up Mr. Dinkles in adorable little outfits for impromptu photo shoots.

Bringing to life the character of Biggie is British actor James Corden, who quickly won over the filmmakers with his take on the character. "I ruined a lot of his takes because I found myself laughing out loud over what he was doing," praises Director Mike Mitchell.

Above and top right: Biggie Expressions • Timothy Lamb; *Right*: Biggie Easy Cry • Willie Real

Top left: Mr. Dinkles Shapes • David Burgess; *Left and above*: Mr. Dinkles • Timothy Lamb; *Below*: Snack Pack Lineup • Willie Real

THE SNACK PACK

During production, key secondary characters started to take shape as the story evolved. While every Troll is Poppy's best friend, there emerged a group of her very, very best Troll friends, which the filmmakers dubbed the Snack Pack. And yes, the term *Snack Pack* foreshadows an ominous plot point in the film! *From left to right:* Creek, Branch, Poppy, Smidge, Fuzzbert, the Fashion Twins, Dinkle, Cooper, Guy Diamond, and DJ Suki.

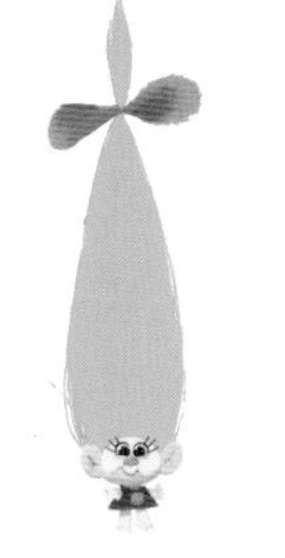

big guy,
easy cry
roughs
happy sad
expressions
big guy
easy cry
expressions
the
lenny
pet
showing
teeth
happy
sad
baby
crying

Opposite page, clockwise from top left: Mr. Dinkles Picture Frame • Avner Geller; Mr. Dinkles Snapshots • *Timothy* Lamb; Biggie and Mr. Dinkles • Willie Real; Big Guy Easy Cry Expressions • Willie Real; Mr. Dinkles Snapshots • Timothy Lamb; *This page:* Biggie and Mr. Dinkles Final Character Renders • DreamWorks Animation

DJ Suki

The Trolls can always count on DJ Suki to get the party started. Relying on natural sounds from the Troll Forest, DJ Suki scratches and mixes noises from crickets, beetles, and other little bugs to create a unique backdrop for the musical moments that take place in Troll Village. Grammy winner Gwen Stefani infuses DJ Suki with her own sense of pop, energy, and style.

This page: DJ Explorations • Willie Real

Top left: DJ • Willie Real; *Bottom left*: DJ Expressions • Willie Real; *Below*: DJ Suki Final Character Render • DreamWorks Animation

Satin & Chenille

The most sartorially minded members of the Snack Pack, Satin (the pink one) and Chenille (the blue one) possess an extensive knowledge of fashion and are instrumental in all Poppy's wardrobe choices for special occasions. Experts in everything from haute couture runways to the latest street trends, these "Fashion Twins" are connected by a loop in their brightly colored hair!

Voiced by the Swedish electropop duo Icona Pop (Caroline Hjelt and Aino Jawo), Satin and Chenille have an almost telepathic bond. "Like Satin and Chenille, Icona Pop literally finish each other's sentences," observes Director Mike Mitchell.

"Harajuku fashion was an inspiration for the twins. We also thought it would be fun if they changed their clothes for every event in the story, like changing into orange prison jumpsuits when captured by the Bergens. But that turned out to be a very costly idea for a running joke."

—Kendal Cronkhite-Shaindlin, Production Designer

Far left: Satin and Chenille • Melissa Kim; *Left and Above*: Fashion Twins Studies • Priscilla Wong; *Right*: Satin and Chenille Final Character Renders • DreamWorks Animation

Top left, top right, middle left, middle right, above, and left: Fashion Twins • Willie Real; *Center:* Fashion Twins • Kendal Cronkhite-Shaindlin

Guy Diamond

In homage to the iconic Troll dolls from the 1960s, the filmmakers decided to include a character sans clothes. "Guy Diamond is our resident 'naked glitter Troll,'" jokes Director Mike Mitchell. Voiced by Kunal Nayyar *(The Big Bang Theory)*, Guy Diamond is a "party on two feet," according to Mitchell, and a Troll who carries himself with his own idea of personal space and an overabundance of self-confidence.

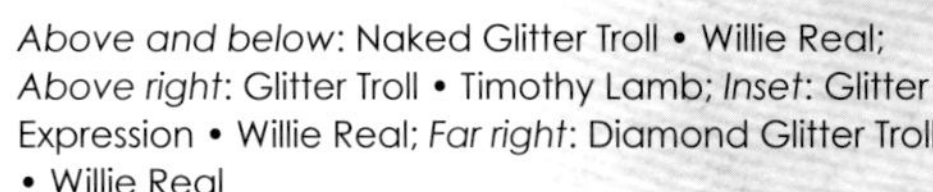

Above and below: Naked Glitter Troll • Willie Real; *Above right*: Glitter Troll • Timothy Lamb; *Inset*: Glitter Expression • Willie Real; *Far right*: Diamond Glitter Troll • Willie Real

Top left: Glitter Troll Facial Expressions • Timothy Lamb; *Bottom left*: Cheerleader Hair • Avner Geller; *Left*: Guy Diamond Final Character Render • DreamWorks Animation

Cooper

A fuzzy giraffelike Troll creature with a permanently plastered grin on his face, Cooper is by far the most peculiar member of the Snack Pack. His boundless enthusiasm makes up for whatever he may lack in the intelligence department.

"Cooper was my favorite to design," admits Art Director/Character Designer Timothy Lamb. "In initial concept art, he was a tap-dancing giraffe, apropos of nothing. I think he was a mailman, too."

As he researched the history of the Troll dolls, Lamb discovered a line of "animal" figures: elephants, turtles, and a giraffe. "The giraffe doll was so funny and haunting to me that I began doing versions based on those toys. I would have been happy if any one of those early concepts made it to the final film, but I think we ended up with the best version in Cooper."

Top row, left to right: Giraffe • Willie Real, Cooper • Timothy Lamb, Giraffe Mailman • Willie Real

Left, above, right, and far right: Cooper Character Studies • Timothy Lamb

Left: Troll Giraffes • Timothy Lamb; *Right*: Cooper Final Character Render • DreamWorks Animation; *Bottom left*: Cooper Facial Expressions • Timothy Lamb

"We have a lot of standout characters for different reasons, but for me personally, I would say Cooper is one of my favorites for his unique design."
—Charles Ellison,
Head of Modeling

Creek

Calm, cool, collected, and capable, Creek channels all his positivity in a somewhat detached, Zen-like manner. Almost too removed, he turns out to be anything but a friend to Poppy and the other Trolls (spoiler alert!).

Creek's dark side manifests when he has to choose between himself and the Troll collective. "We needed someone who caused Poppy to question her positive attitude," explains Director Mike Mitchell. "When Creek sells out the Trolls to Chef in order to save himself, that provides a very important turning point for Poppy."

This page: Creek Character Studies • Timothy Lamb

Above: Creek Character Studies • Timothy Lamb; *Right*: Creek Final Character Render • DreamWorks Animation; *Below*: Creek Poses • Timothy Lamb

Smidge

Smidge is a teeny-tiny Troll with a shockingly deep baritone voice, courtesy of Co-Director Walt Dohrn. Her hobbies include weightlifting, listening to Swedish death metal, and crocheting. "What makes the character work so well is that she just pops in—in the most random, hilarious moments," says Dohrn.

Top left: Smidge Color Tests • Timothy Lamb; *Top middle*: Smidge Expressions • Willie Real; *Above*: Smidge Expressions • Timothy Lamb; *Far right*: Smidge Final Character Render • DreamWorks Animation

Fuzzbert

An enigma wrapped in a riddle, Fuzzbert is a Troll made entirely of hair. "We sometimes wonder what's inside," says Director Mike Mitchell. "You could probably find anything you need, sort of like Snoopy's doghouse."

Fuzzbert communicates with the other Trolls using guttural noises. "He clicks, clacks and grunts throughout the film as if everyone understands him, which they do," says Co-Director Walt Dohrn, who voiced the character.

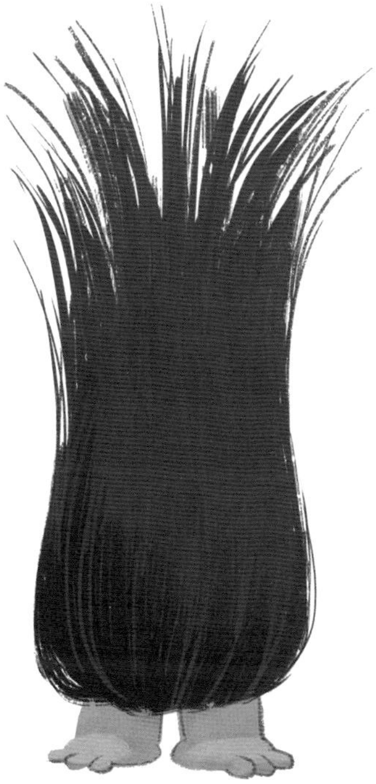

Above: Fuzzbert • Timothy Lamb; *Right:* Fuzzbert Final Character Render • DreamWorks Animation; *Below:* Town Hall • Danny Langston

"Fuzzbert is just hair and feet."
—Mike Mitchell, Director

Above: Kazoo • Priscilla Wong; *Right:* Fuzzbert • Timothy Lamb

King Peppy

As the brave leader of the Trolls, King Peppy led his people on a torch-lit escape from Bergen-town decades ago. His heroism and valor are the stuff of Troll legend. Quick with inspirational words of wisdom, King Peppy ushered in a new era of happiness and security in Troll Village. Now, twenty years later, King Peppy is ready to pass the torch to his daughter, Poppy.

Right: King Peppy • Timothy Lamb; *Top right*: Lighting Key • Avner Geller; *Far right*: Old Peppy • Timothy Lamb; *Below*: Peppy Stages • Timothy Lamb

"The most exciting thing about this film is that it doesn't look like CG. It looks hand-made, and the result is incredibly inspiring."
—Walt Dohrn,
Co-Director

Far left: King Peppy • Joel Crawford; *Left*: King Peppy Final Character Render • DreamWorks Animation

Grandma Rosiepuff

In a flashback sequence, the film explores an early memory of Branch's—one that is not so pleasant. But it does give us a glimpse into understanding why Branch is the way he is.

One day, as a young Troll, Branch was singing to his heart's content without a care in the world. He was so engrossed in his music that he neglected to notice an approaching Bergen. "The Bergen made a move to grab Branch, but brave Rosiepuff pushed Branch out of the way in time, but she was snatched," explains Producer Gina Shay.

Naturally, it was a traumatic and defining moment for the young Troll. Branch decided that he would never sing again, subjecting himself to live a lonely existence in his fear bunker.

Designed by Art Director/Character Designer Timothy Lamb, Grandma Rosiepuff is the epitome of what every grandma should be: doting, adorable, and lovable. "Branch's Grandma Rosiepuff is one of our favorite designs," says Director Mike Mitchell. "She's pretty much the grandma that every Troll wants as their own."

The design of Grandma Rosiepuff was reworked from a design of the film's original turncoat villain, Miss Guffin. Explains Producer Gina Shay, "Miss Guffin was Poppy's mentor who turned on her at the end of the second act. We set her up as so appealing and funny that nobody could recover when she turned evil." As development progressed, Creek took on the role of the turncoat and Miss Guffin became Grandma Rosiepuff.

Above right: Miss Guffin Expressions • Timothy Lamb;
Right: Miss Guffin Color Studies • Timothy Lamb

"Branch's Grandma Rosiepuff is one our favorite designs. She's pretty much the grandma that every Troll wants as their own."
—Mike Mitchell, Director

Top left and above: Miss Guffin Character Studies • Timothy Lamb; *Center*: Miss Guffin Profile • Craig Kellman; *Left*: Miss Guffin Character Studies • Craig Kellman; *Right*: Grandma Rosiepuff Final Character Render • DreamWorks Animation; *Above*: Miss Guffin Character Study • Timothy Lamb

Troll Villagers

Left: Painter Troll • Willie Real; Above: Painter Troll • Timothy Lamb; Right: Harper Final Character Render • DreamWorks Animation

HARPER Quvenzhané Wallis voices the Trolls' resident artist and painter, Harper, designed by Art Director/Character Designer Timothy Lamb. "Harper uses her puff of hair as a paintbrush," explains Producer Gina Shay. "She has a white smock that she manages to keep clean, but her whole body is one big splatter painting."

Below: Skitterboards • Timothy Lamb; Right: Aspen Heitz Final Character Render • DreamWorks Animation

KARMA Designed by Character Designer Willie Real, Karma is scientifically inclined and has an inquisitive mind—she's always on the lookout for new wonders of the natural world.

Left: Karma Final Character Render • DreamWorks Animation; Right: Science Troll Expressions • Willie Real

ASPEN HEITZ As his name implies, Aspen Heitz loves to climb the tallest trees in Troll Village and the surrounding forest. His closest friends are the bugs that inhabit the treetops. A skilled skitterboarder, Aspen can perform the jaw-dropping skitter trick known as "the double rainbow."

CYBIL A master yogi, Cybil was created early on in the film development process but was ultimately cut when Creek took on a larger role in the narrative. "A lot the yoga/ Zen elements from Cybil were later incorporated into Creek's character," explains Art Director/Character Designer Timothy Lamb.

Clockwise from far left: Maddy Final Character Render • DreamWorks Animation; Hairstylist Troll • Willie Real; Cybil Final Character Render • DreamWorks Animation; Guru Troll • Willie Real

MADDY As Poppy's personal stylist, image consultant, and cosmetologist, Maddy always keeps Poppy ahead of the latest hair and makeup trends.

Troll Creatures

Far left, middle: Defibrillator Beetles • Timothy Lamb; *Far left, bottom*: Forest Creatures • Amélie Fléchais; *Below*: Critters • Timothy Lamb; *Bottom*: Caterpillar • Timothy Lamb

Designed by Art Director/Character Designer Timothy Lamb, the creatures that coexist with the Trolls complement their cohabitants in every way. "The creatures Timothy designed are so colorful, happy, and uniquely weird," praises Co-Director Walt Dohrn.

"The design of Biggie's pet worm, Mr. Dinkles, actually informed the overall direction and tone of all the Troll creatures," explains Lamb. "Once we had the design of Mr. Dinkles locked, we were able to create a world of creatures that all fit within the same design aesthetic and shape language."

Common design elements include the glitter eyeball without an iris or pupil and color schemes similar to those used for the Trolls. But the art department made sure to differentiate the creatures sufficiently so they wouldn't compete with the Trolls when they were in the same scene.

Including the creatures featured in Sequence 1100 *(see pages 84-85)*, Lamb designed nearly fifty crazy, wacky, and wonderful Troll creatures for the film.

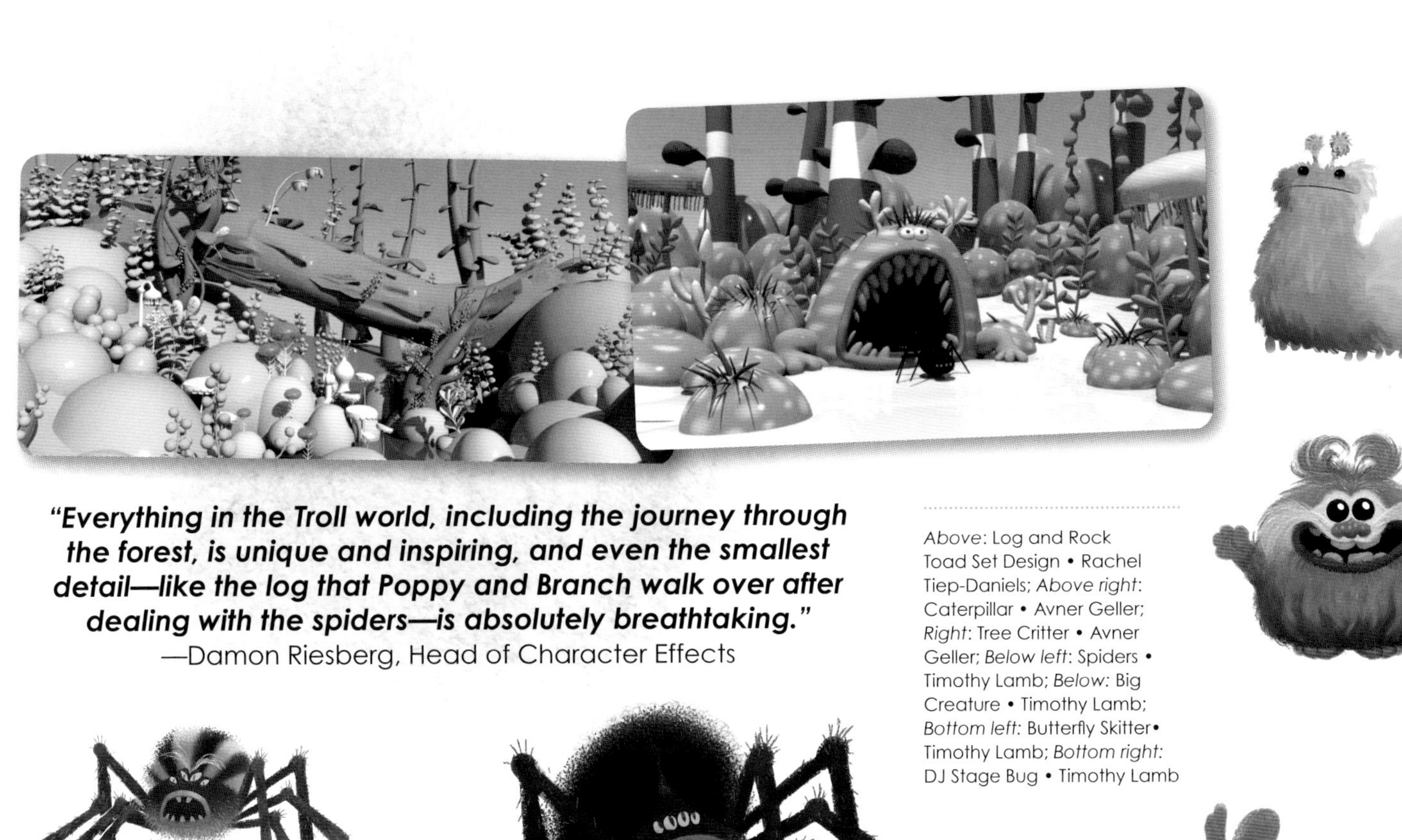

"Everything in the Troll world, including the journey through the forest, is unique and inspiring, and even the smallest detail—like the log that Poppy and Branch walk over after dealing with the spiders—is absolutely breathtaking."
—Damon Riesberg, Head of Character Effects

Above: Log and Rock Toad Set Design • Rachel Tiep-Daniels; *Above right*: Caterpillar • Avner Geller; *Right*: Tree Critter • Avner Geller; *Below left*: Spiders • Timothy Lamb; *Below:* Big Creature • Timothy Lamb; *Bottom left:* Butterfly Skitter• Timothy Lamb; *Bottom right:* DJ Stage Bug • Timothy Lamb

The Trolls' World

Left: Flower Props • Sebastien Piquet; *Below*: Troll Village Concept • Amélie Fléchais; *Opposite, top*: Troll Village • Ritchie Sacilioc; *Opposite, bottom*: Troll Village Fiber Sculpture • Sayuri Sasaki Hemann, photograph by Samantha Trauben

For the design and look of the world of the Trolls, the filmmakers started with a blank slate. Early inspiration came from the era that marked the height of popularity for the original Troll dolls—the groovy world of the 1970s.

"The directors, Kendal [Cronkhite-Shaindlin, production designer], and I all grew up in the '70s," explains Producer Gina Shay, "so we were all locked into the idea that we wanted to honor the moments we had with our Trolls as children, but also tap into the heritage of the dolls' Scandinavian origins. Kendal artfully fused elements of Scandinavian design with handmade qualities of the '70s and created a new fairy-tale look."

As the story developed, the filmmakers realized that the Trolls were more than just inhabitants of the forest—they were an integral part of the ecosystem. Explains Cronkhite-Shaindlin, "The Trolls are a vital part of the forest, creatures living in harmony with their surroundings, so it made sense for their fuzzy textures, round, plump shape-language, and Scandinavian design to be incorporated into the environment."

While researching looks for the world of the Trolls, an artist in Cronkhite-Shaindlin's department referred her to the work of French children's book illustrator Amélie Fléchais. Known for her use of vibrant colors and whimsical character designs, Fléchais has quickly become a sought-after talent, having most recently provided conceptual and visual design artwork for the Academy Award–nominated film *Song of the Sea*.

"I asked Amélie if she would be interested in doing some concept work for the film and, to our delight, she said yes," recalls Cronkhite-Shaindlin. Fléchais contributed about a dozen visual development pieces to the film.

Once the visual style of the Trolls' world was decided, the crew began exploring how to translate that look into 3D. An important first step was to combine the whimsical style of Fléchais's illustrations with fiber art techniques and bring all that together in CG. Collaborating with Sayuri Sasaki Hemann—a self-described "multidisciplinary artist" who works in various textiles, including felt, organza, wool, and fiber—was the answer.

Inspired by the way light is reflected off the surface of each medium, Hemann "created a beautiful, permanent installation for the Portland airport of a jellyfish tank completely constructed with fibers, fabric, and felt," praises Cronkhite-Shaindlin. "Not only is it mesmerizing to watch in motion, but her material choices and sense of color are breathtaking!"

Cronkhite-Shaindlin contacted Hemann, who is based in Iowa City, and pitched her the idea of creating a model of the Troll Forest completely out of fiber. Working off the visual development art from Amélie Fléchais, Hemann spent about a month dyeing fibers and fabrics to get the right colors for depicting the world of the Trolls. Explains Cronkhite-Shaindlin, "She used a number of felting, knitting, macramé, and sewing techniques to create an amazing piece of art!"

Just as excited as the film crew, Hemann drove her creation from Iowa City to the PDI/DreamWorks campus in Redwood City, California, where she met the crew in person.

According to Cronkhite-Shaindlin, Hemann's "fiber forest" jump-started the crew's design process. "Fiber art, slow art, and anything handmade became our big sources of reference along with Scandinavian design and the 1970s," says Cronkhite-Shaindlin. "Every department responsible for creating this world in CG poured over the model, analyzing all aspects of it."

"For Troll Village and the surrounding forest, we chose to keep the palette limited to soft greens and blues with dappled sunlight, so that our colorful Trolls would be the accent in their world."
—Timothy Lamb, Art Director/Character Designer

"What Kendal [Cronkhite-Shaindlin] has done is create a whole forest and applied different textures to everything."
—Walt Dohrn, Co-Director

Above and below: Sequence 200
Static Area Layout • Sebastien Piquet

Above: Troll Forest • Sebastien Piquet; *Right*: Sequence 200 Set Layout • Sebastien Piquet; *Below*: Troll Characters Posing • Sebastien Piquet

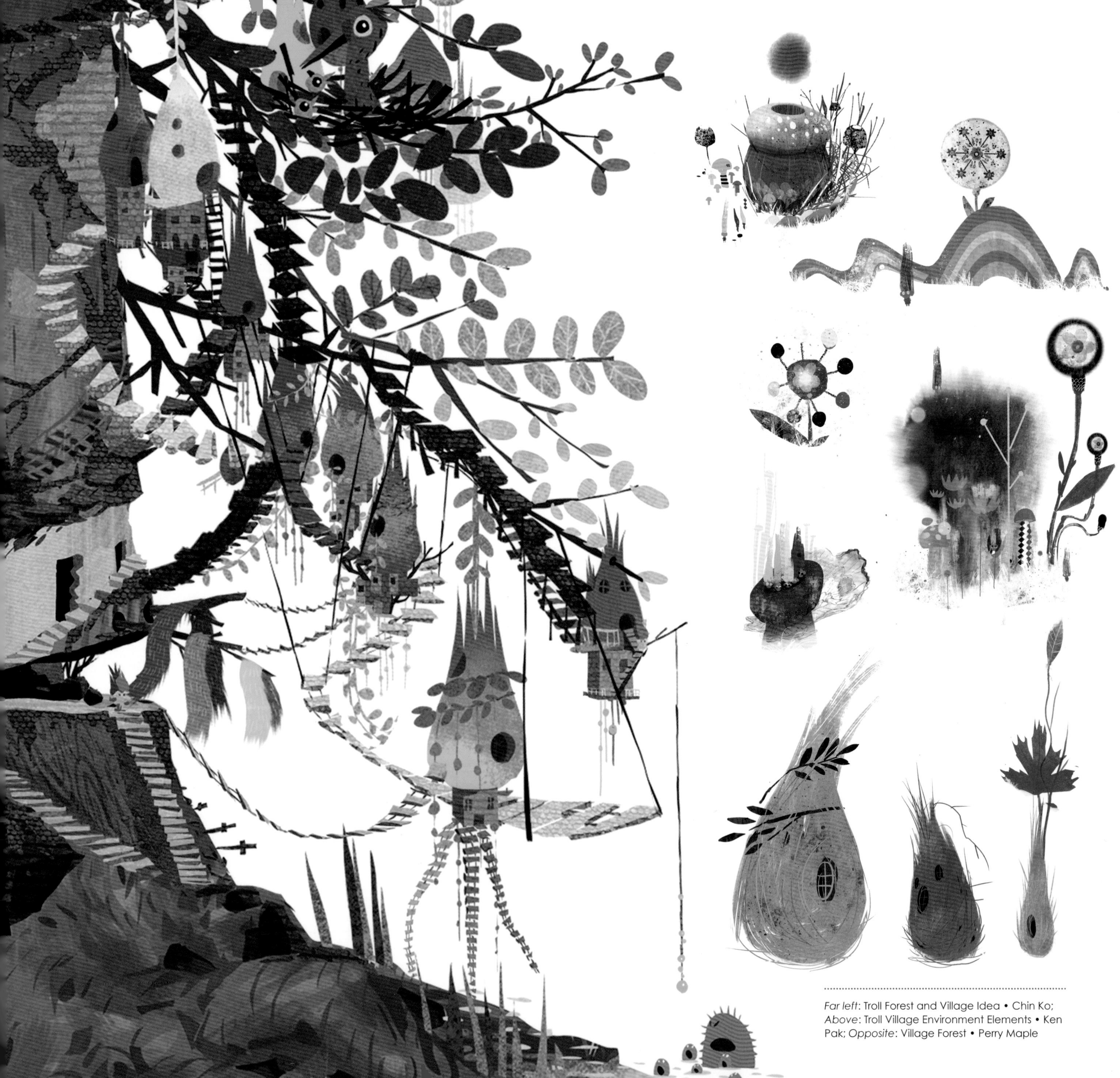

Far left: Troll Forest and Village Idea • Chin Ko; *Above*: Troll Village Environment Elements • Ken Pak; *Opposite*: Village Forest • Perry Maple

POPPY'S HOUSE The Trolls build everything from their hair, including their houses, bridges, trampolines, and zip lines, and make them look like integral parts of their environment. Such is the case with Poppy's house (and every Troll's house, for that matter). What appears to be a pod dangling from a tree branch, is actually a "house" made of fibers and hairs that opens up like a blossom, revealing a dwelling space. "We wanted to make sure that everything in the forest blended in with its surroundings and looked like it belonged to the ecosystem," says producer Gina Shay.

Top: Poppy's House • Carlos Felipe León; *Bottom:* Fashion Twins' House • Priscilla Wong

FASHION TWINS' POD The house pod of the Fashion Twins Satin and Chenille is Poppy's go-to sanctuary when she needs the latest look. Stocked with rolls of fabric, yarn, ribbon, thread, and garments, the Fashion Twins' pod is where all Troll fashion trends begin.

AEROBICS AREA Like everything else in Troll Village, workouts are based around organic elements that help cultivate Troll well-being. "Naturally, your standard workout focuses on building the core hair follicles that are crucial for all Trolls," explains Director Mike Mitchell.

Top: Aerobics Area • Carlos Felipe León; *Bottom:* Dance Pod Lighting Key • Peter Zaslav

DANCE PODS Every day is a party in Troll Village. And what party doesn't have a dance floor? Designed to give perspective and depth, each dance pod features a different group of Trolls doing what they do best: singing and dancing!

Branch's Fear Bunker

The paranoid and reclusive Branch lives about as far away from the rest of the Trolls as he can get. "He's like the weirdo that lives on the edge of town," explains Production Designer Kendal Cronkhite-Shaindlin.

Because he lives in a constant state of fear, believing that the Bergens will return at any moment, Branch has gone underground. Literally. Finding refuge under a giant rock, he's built himself a "fear bunker" stocked with enough supplies to last him ten years.

The fear bunker is actually an impressive and complex network of nooks and crannies designed to keep Branch safe. Artist Amélie Fléchais created a cross-section view of Branch's bunker in an early visual development piece for this set. This became the inspiration for all the cutaway views of the underground homes and tunnels in the film. "I've always been interested in cross-section perspectives on sets," admits Director Mike Mitchell.

For inspiration, he looked to the innovative set designs of films such as *The Ladies Man* and *The Life Aquatic*. "The cutaway view of the inner workings of Branch's bunker, in particular the elevator, was a perfect opportunity to continue the film language we'd developed for the Trolls' universe," explains Mitchell.

The story team and artists used the cutaway technique later in the film when the Trolls escape through the root tunnel and again in Bridget's emotional journey downstairs to her basement/dishwashing dungeon.

When Branch's worst nightmare comes true with the arrival of Chef, Poppy escapes to his bunker. She desperately tries to persuade him to join her, but he refuses. At first.

Once Poppy invites all the Trolls in the village to take refuge in Branch's fear bunker, Branch is faced with two choices: stay in the bunker with all the Trolls or venture out with Poppy on a rescue mission. He chooses the latter.

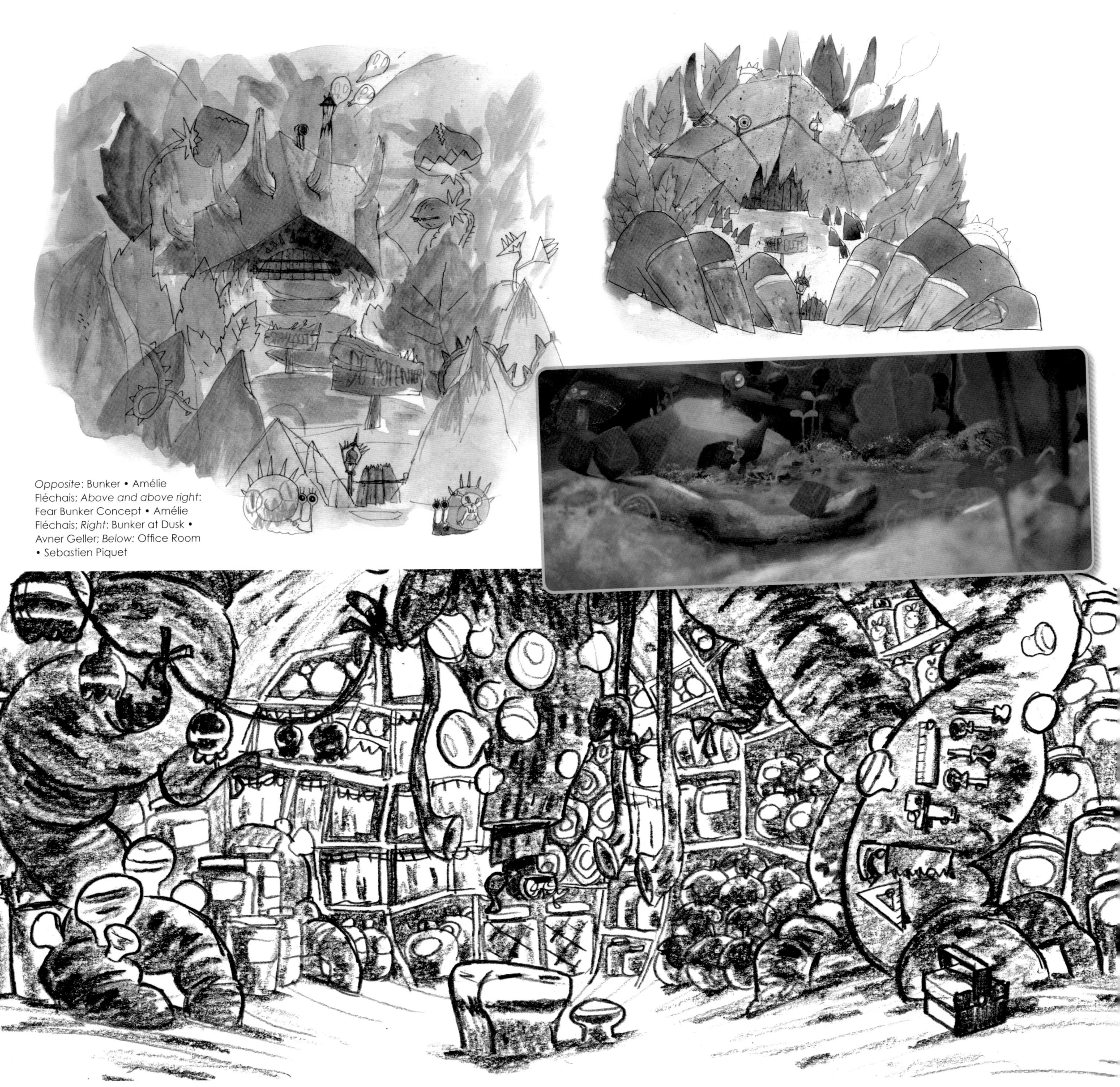

Opposite: Bunker • Amélie Fléchais; *Above and above right*: Fear Bunker Concept • Amélie Fléchais; *Right*: Bunker at Dusk • Avner Geller; *Below:* Office Room • Sebastien Piquet

Poppy's Journey

Determined to find and rescue her friends, Poppy sets out on a journey into the unknown that takes her from Troll Village to Bergentown.

On the way, she and Branch pass through many diverse, crazy places. To depict these transitional spaces, the artists had to find a way to change the design of the environments gradually while staying true to the world of the Trolls and the overall design aesthetic set by Production Designer Kendal Cronkhite-Shaindlin. "There are twenty-seven different places that Poppy travels through," explains Director Mike Mitchell. "Each of the locations incorporates only two colors. What Kendal, Tim [Lamb], [Visual Development Artists] Sebastien Piquet and Avner Geller accomplished is amazing."

Poppy's journey ends at the beautiful spider web/log set designed by Visual Development Artist Rachel Tiep-Daniels with color and light by Sebastien Piquet.

Above: Poppy Stages • Timothy Lamb; *Left* and *below left*: Leaving Troll Village Color Keys • Timothy Lamb; *Below*: Troll Snapshot • Timothy Lamb; *Bottom*: Journey Moment • Sebastien Piquet

Above: Poppy Stages • Timothy Lamb; *Left*: Tentacle sketches • Sebastien Piquet and Timothy Lamb; *Below*: Wind • Avner Geller; *Bottom*: Color Yarn Hill • Sebastien Piquet

Opposite, left: Travel Concept • Amélie Fléchais; *Opposite, top right*: Troll Snapshot • Timothy Lamb; *Opposite, bottom right*: Branch with Footprint • Amélie Fléchais; *Top*: Fire Plant • Timothy Lamb and Sebastien Piquet; *Above*: Mom Bird and Baby Birds • Timothy Lamb; *Left*: Exploring Birds • Sebastien Piquet

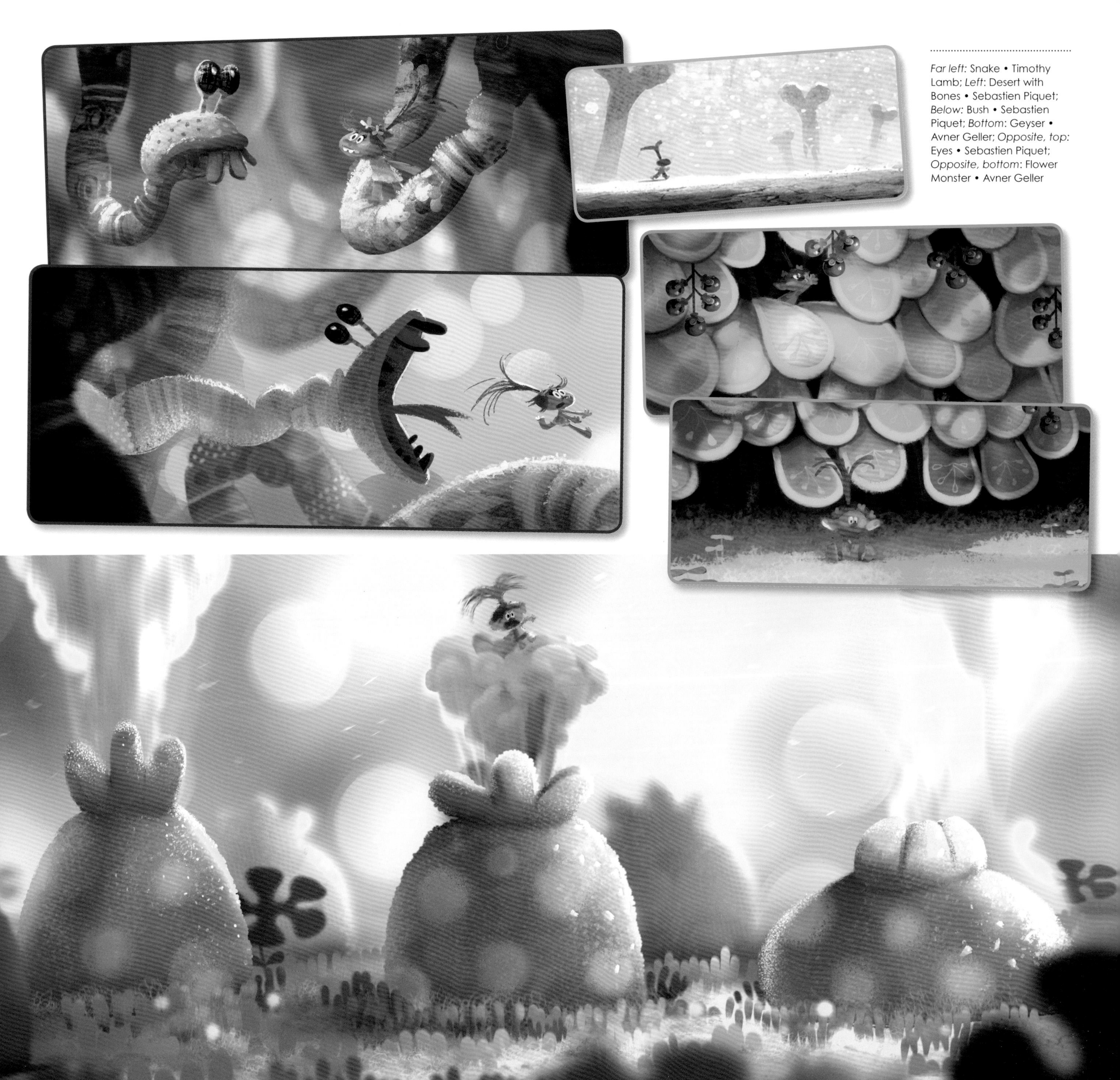

Far left: Snake • Timothy Lamb; *Left*: Desert with Bones • Sebastien Piquet; *Below:* Bush • Sebastien Piquet; *Bottom*: Geyser • Avner Geller; *Opposite, top:* Eyes • Sebastien Piquet; *Opposite, bottom*: Flower Monster • Avner Geller

Clockwise from left: Exploring Rain • Sebastien Piquet; Exploring Rain B • Sebastien Piquet; Rain Plop • Sebastien Piquet; Winter • Sebastien Piquet; Crystal Cave • Timothy Lamb; Sketches • Sebastien Piquet; *Opposite, Top*: Hill Monster • Avner Geller; *Opposite, Bottom*: Hill Monster B • Avner Geller

Color Script

This page: Color Script (Sampling) • Peter Zaslav, Avner Geller, Timothy Lamb, Sebastien Piquet, and Zhaoping Wei

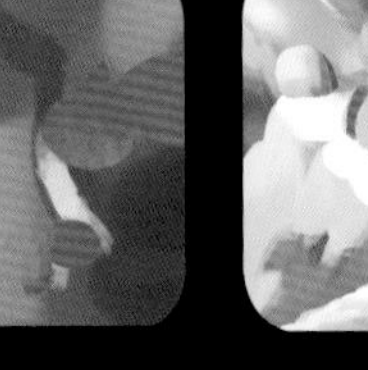

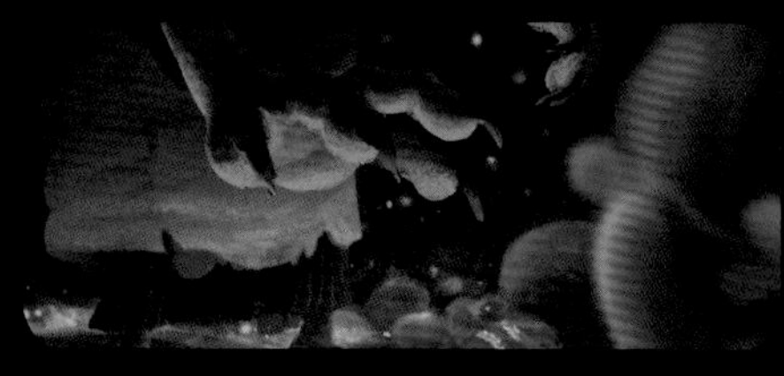

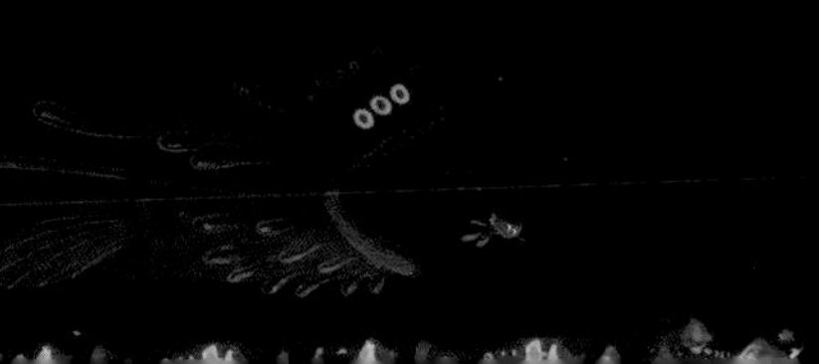
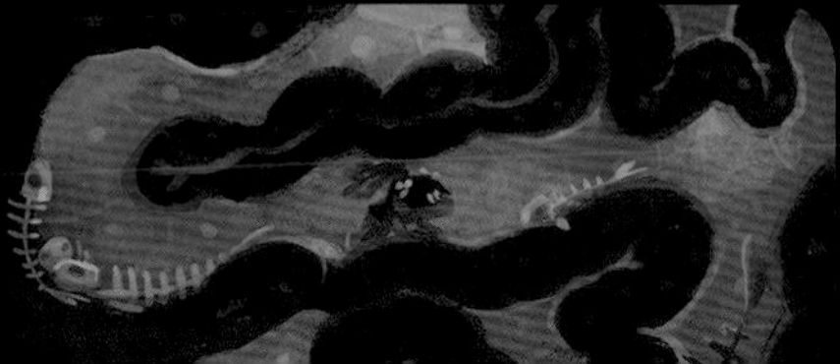

SEQUENCE 1100

Silence, Saturated

Toward the end of their journey, Poppy and Branch decide to make camp for the night and get some rest before their final trek into Bergentown. It is during this sequence that we, the audience, get to see just how different Poppy and Branch are from one another: the eternally upbeat and positive Poppy contrasts quite markedly with the ill-tempered grouch who is very (happily?) set in his ways.

Recalls Producer Gina Shay, "In the early days of breaking the story for *Trolls*, we wanted to create a moment that juxtaposed Branch and Poppy's contrasting personalities. We thought of all of the exemplary moments in classic film history to inspire us."

"It is a great moment in the film—we get to see Branch and Poppy's opposite viewpoints of the world perfectly on display," says Supervising Animator Mark Donald.

To design the sizable supporting cast of creatures in the scene, the filmmakers looked to both iconic and contemporary artists for inspiration. "We turned to the designs and look of Miyazaki's world and characters," says Director Mike Mitchell, referring the master of Japanese animation, Hayao Miyazaki.

Adds Co-Director Walt Dohrn, "We also turned to the amazing world seen in *Adventure Time* for inspiration."

At the start of the sequence, you don't even notice these background characters. Explains Art Director/ Character Designer Timothy Lamb, "Most of the designs were developed with the idea that they needed to first be camouflaged and then emerge from the forest with colorful bioluminescence."

As Poppy begins to sing and the scene unfolds, the forest comes to full-color life. "We didn't hold back on the color choices," continues Lamb. "Saturation was our friend in giving this scene its kaleidoscopic effect." To achieve the desired look, the artists based the effect on fluorescent paint that was lit with spotlights in a dark environment—not blacklight, but fluorescent. Visual Development Artist Avner Geller brought the scene to life with his image of the chorus of creatures singing with Poppy.

For Lamb, the biggest challenge with the scene was keeping each character's design simple, quickly readable, and appealing. "I found that the more complex a design was, the more threatening the character became," he says. "With a collection of such diverse creatures, I knew that we needed to design starting with clear geometric shapes so that the complexity wouldn't spin out of control."

One other detail that Mitchell added to the sequence is the photos of the missing Snack Pack members (adorned in a very Poppy-crafty way with popsicle stick frames and stickers), which she displays around her sleeping bag. In a very touching moment, she bids goodnight to each of her friends, much to the annoyance of Branch, who just wants to sleep.

But sleep will have to wait for Branch. When he demands silence from Poppy, that's her cue to launch into her very own rendition of Simon & Garfunkel's "The Sound of Silence," which emerges in a psychedelic cacophony of sound, light, color, and character. "Singing is her secret weapon when she is feeling down and missing her friends," says Supervising Animator Mark Donald. "So she imposes this positivity on Branch whether he likes it or not. We really feel the harmony that the Trolls have with their surroundings when Poppy brings the forest alive to join in her song." Adds Director Mike Mitchell, "She's a quirky twist on Snow White or Cinderella, who are friendly with all the forest creatures."

With myriad forest creatures serving as backup, the end result is nothing short of sensory overload as the supporting cast comes to take up practically every inch of the scene's final frame. "I like to call the last shot of the sequence a 'Timothy Lamb Extravaganza'!" says Director Mike Mitchell.

Previous pages: Silence Serenade • Avner Geller; *Left*: Branch • Avner Geller; *Top*: Sequence 1100 Color Keys • Peter Zaslav

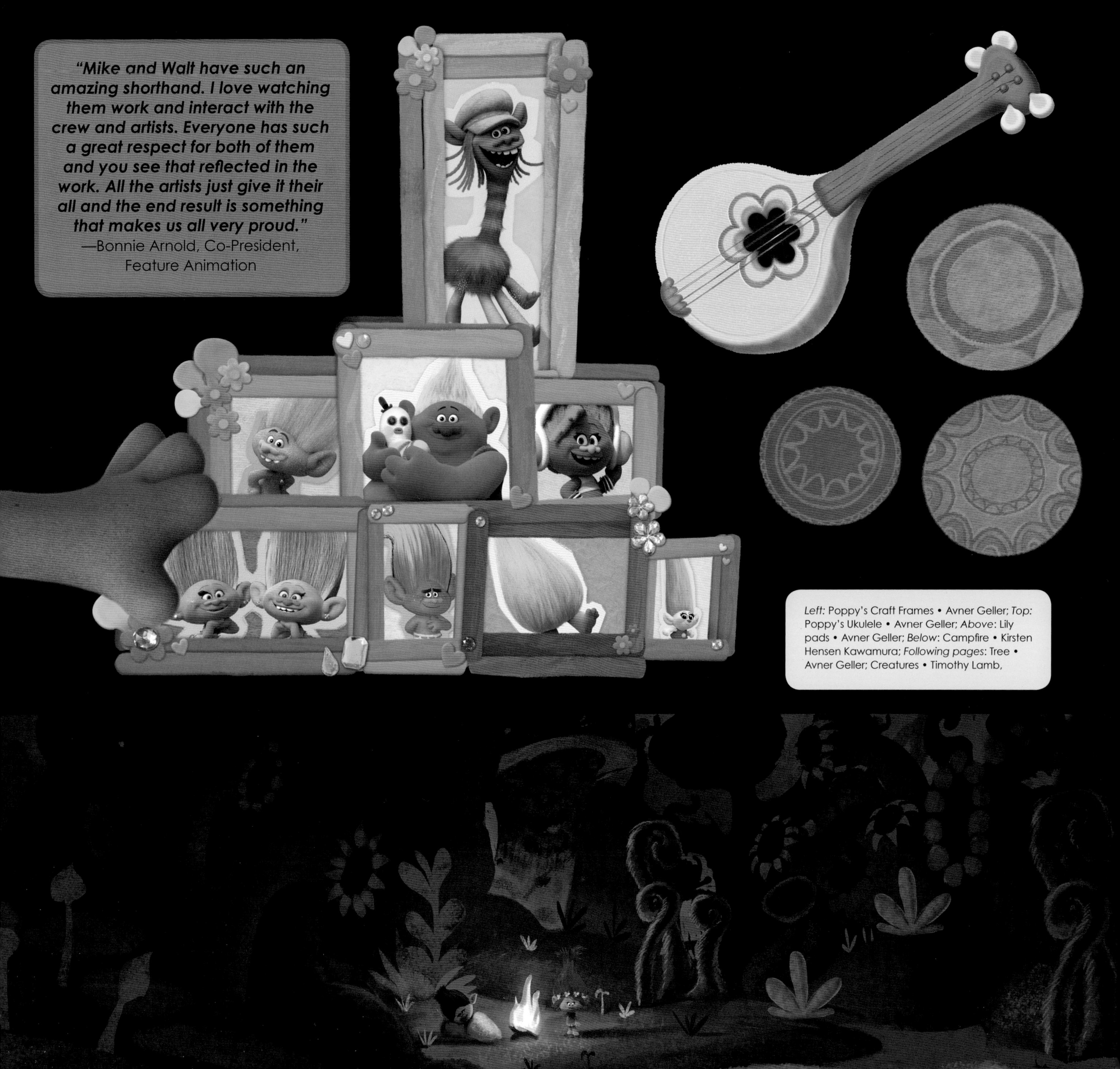

"Mike and Walt have such an amazing shorthand. I love watching them work and interact with the crew and artists. Everyone has such a great respect for both of them and you see that reflected in the work. All the artists just give it their all and the end result is something that makes us all very proud."
—Bonnie Arnold, Co-President, Feature Animation

Left: Poppy's Craft Frames • Avner Geller; *Top:* Poppy's Ukulele • Avner Geller; *Above*: Lily pads • Avner Geller; *Below*: Campfire • Kirsten Hensen Kawamura; *Following pages*: Tree • Avner Geller; Creatures • Timothy Lamb,

Story

The sequence plays so well largely due to the well-crafted storyboards from Head of Story Joel Crawford and his team. "The sequence encapsulates the essence of the entire story of *Trolls*," says Crawford, "and how their happiness ultimately brings out the joy in the world around them."

When the story team set out to storyboard the sequence, one of the biggest challenges they faced was the sheer number of forest creatures that populate the scene. Explains Story Artist Tim Heitz, "There is a lot going on, and the music clip is actually quite short, so I think the biggest challenge for us was fitting in as many entertaining creature moments as possible into such a tiny time frame. I would have been happy extending the song and trying to fit in twenty or thirty more of those guys!"

"I knew we were going to be checking in with Branch a couple of times throughout the song to see his reaction and that most of the 'singing creatures' would be backing up Poppy, so I had the idea to make this little spider drop down next to Branch and whisper 'hello' in his ear and then for Branch to flick him away. I was happy to see him make the cut and somehow he became a recurring character throughout the movie!"

—Tim Heitz, Story Artist

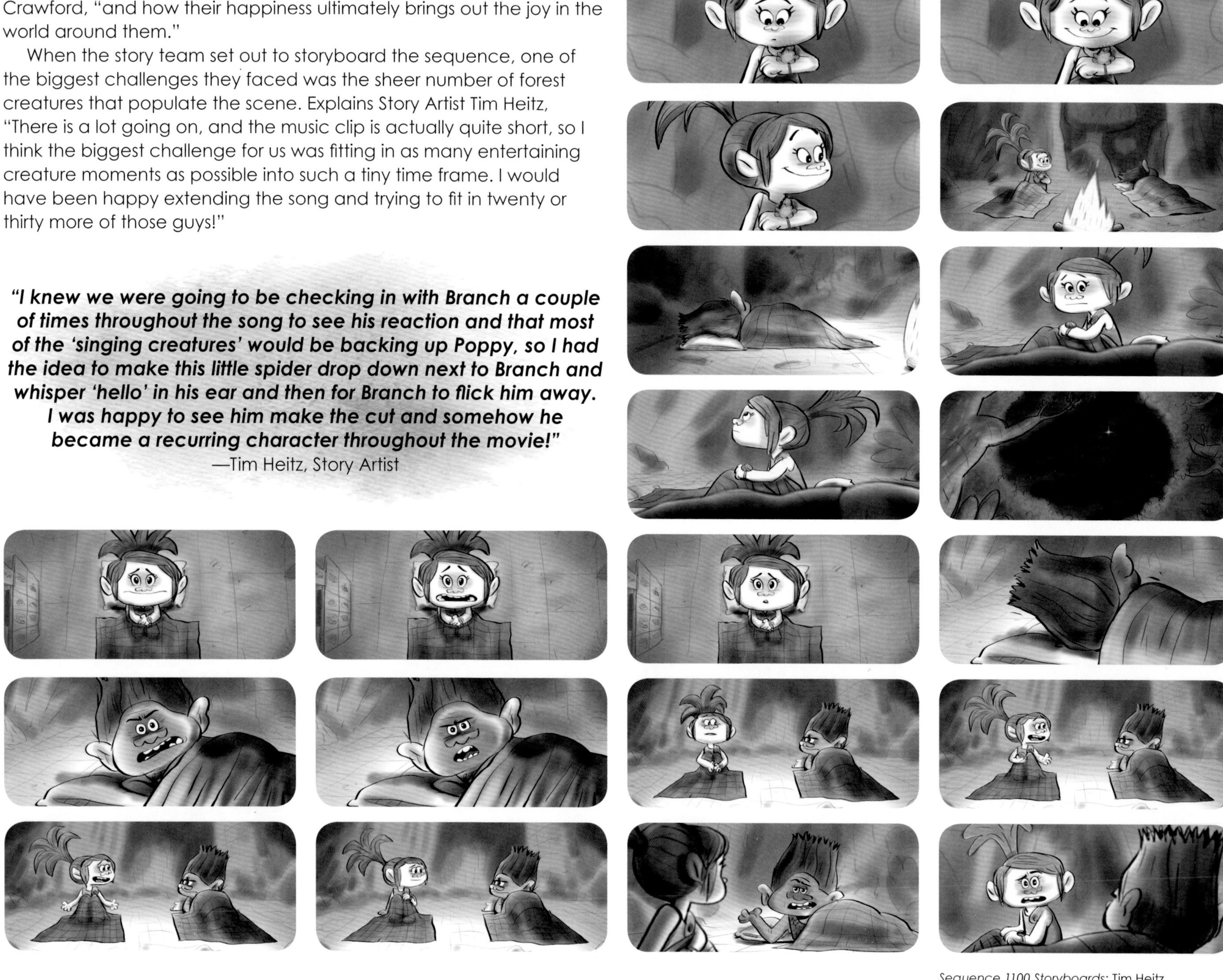

Sequence 1100 Storyboards: Tim Heitz

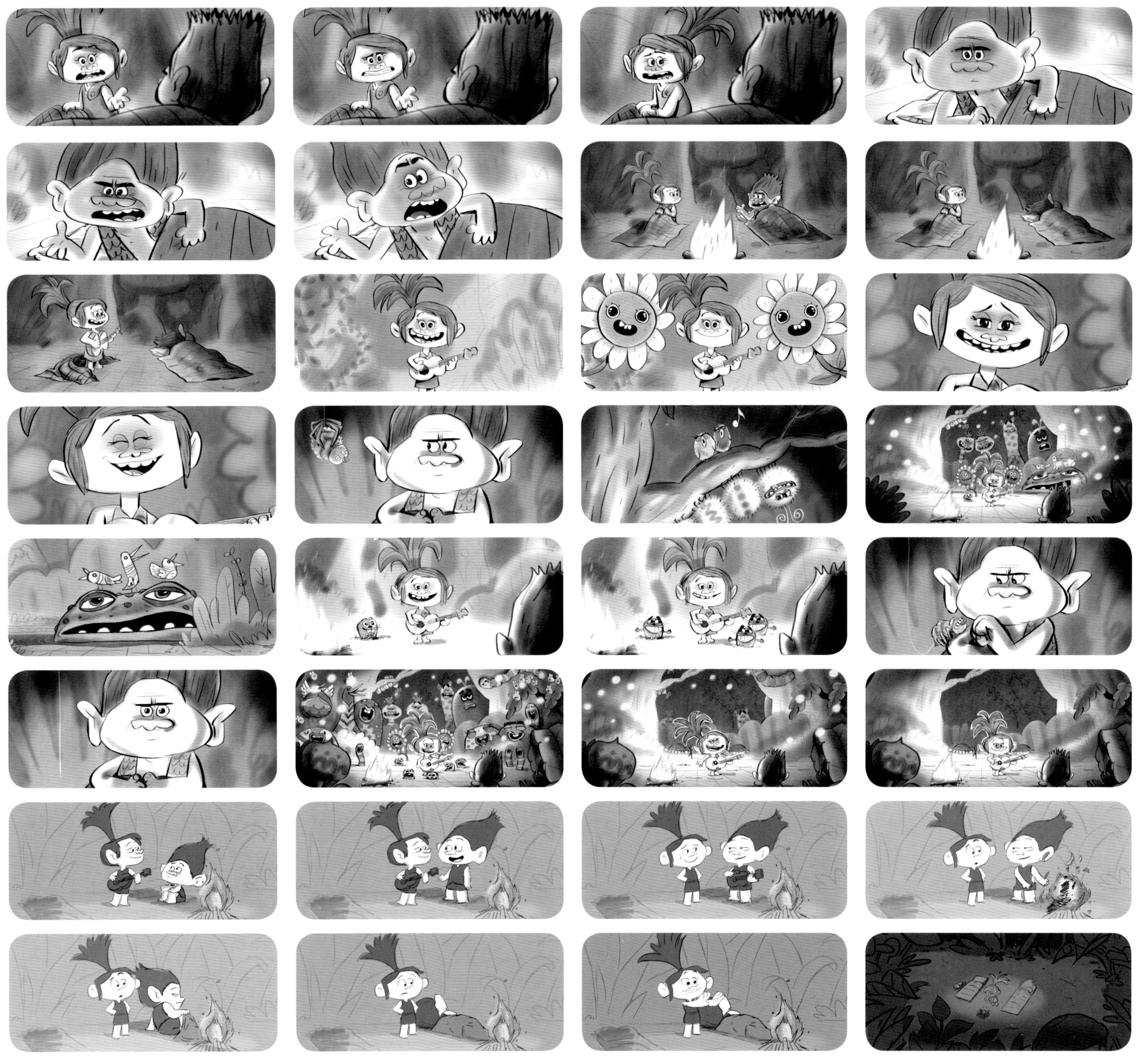

Layout

For the layout department (often referred to as the camera/cinematography department), Sequence 1100 was approached as a film-within-a-film. "Since this sequence contains a beginning, a middle, and an end, we treated the entire scene as a short film," explains Head of Rough Layout Yong Duk Jhun. "The cinematography had to be subtle at the beginning, then build to a more exciting and interesting dynamic in the middle, and move back toward a more subtle approach to play out the comedy."

The layout team had to pay especially close attention when all the creatures start to sing. "That moment had to have lots of energy and rhythm at the same time and needed to be organic to the story," continues Jhun. "It eventually worked out quite well, but it was not easy to find the right balance between excitement and subtlety."

This page: Rough layout by Victor Robert, Jotham Herzon, Pamela B. Stefan, John W. McInnis, and Dorian Bustamante; set dressing by Rachel Lagdao and David Patrick Valera

"I think [Sequence 1100] is one of my favorite sequences in the film because it is so full of fantasy and whimsy. You are not quite sure if it really is happening as you are watching it."
—Sandy Kao, Head of Rigging/Character Technical Director

Modeling

One of the biggest challenges the modeling department faced in Sequence 1100 was that all the creatures play an integral role in composing the space. "Usually you worry about an environment as its own entity, accounting for scale, acting space, things like that," offers Head of Modeling Charles Ellison.

In the case of Sequence 1100, the creatures needed to create a very specific composition. Piecing it all together meant the modelers tasked with creating the creatures and those building the environment had to work closely with one another, as well as continuously provide context so that the production designer, art director, and layout team could stay aligned with the direction.

"I think the biggest challenge was in creating creatures whose shape language in general was so simple," says Ellison. "We had to think as simple as we could for the shapes of the creatures and anticipate what the fur and surfacing were going to add."

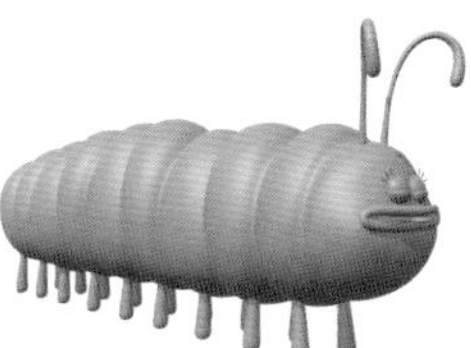

"This sequence captures so much of what makes our movie fun, quirky, and unique. Artistically, it demonstrates the style and tone of the film."
—Charles Ellison, Head of Modeling

Top: Caterpillar • Sean Choi; *Above, left to right*: Flower • Abraham Meneu Oset; Browbug • Abraham Meneu Oset; Squirrel • Abraham Meneu Oset; Puffbug • Abraham Meneu Oset; Plant Puffbug • Abraham Meneu Oset; Spider • Abraham Meneu Oset: Flower Groups • *Bottom, left to right*: Flower • Abraham Meneu Oset; Fish • Sean Choi; Worm • Sean Choi

Rigging

Rigging, for the uninitiated, is basically the mechanics that allow the animators to move the characters. "Think of 'rigging' as the strings that move the puppet or, in our case, the characters," explains Co-Producer Holly Edwards.

While the rigs for *Trolls* were not terribly complex, there were a lot of them, especially in Sequence 1100. "Since there were so many creatures, and most of them are in the same shots, we had to make sure that they were all delivered to animation on time," explains Head of Rigging/Character Technical Director Sandy Kao. "We wanted to ensure that the expectations of the animation team were met for every individual creature so that it could do what it needed to do in the sequence."

In order to animate as many characters as possible, the rigging department worked with the art and modeling departments to determine the best way to maximize the number of characters by breaking away from traditional character-rigging practices. "We relied heavily on shapes already modeled with very simple controls for animation," says Kao. "They were all fairly simple rigs but a few, like the fish, had a few more controls so they could do things like have their lips quiver as they sing."

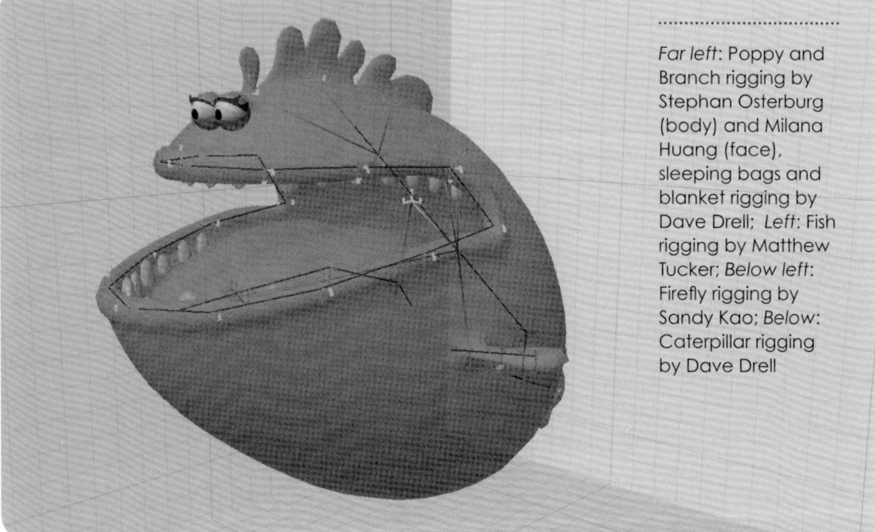

Far left: Poppy and Branch rigging by Stephan Osterburg (body) and Milana Huang (face), sleeping bags and blanket rigging by Dave Drell; *Left*: Fish rigging by Matthew Tucker; *Below left*: Firefly rigging by Sandy Kao; *Below*: Caterpillar rigging by Dave Drell

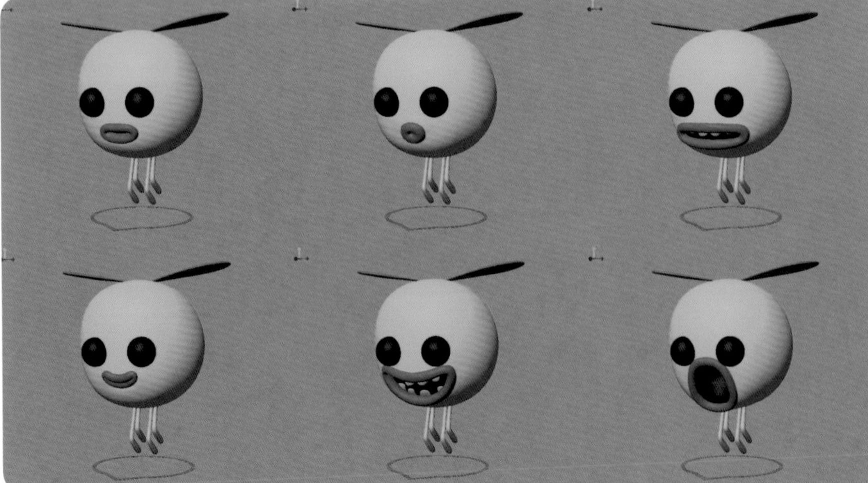

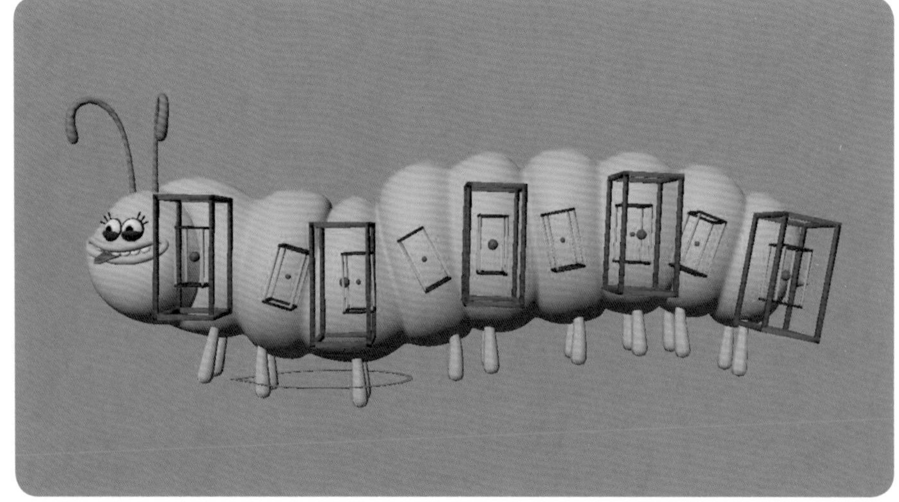

Surfacing

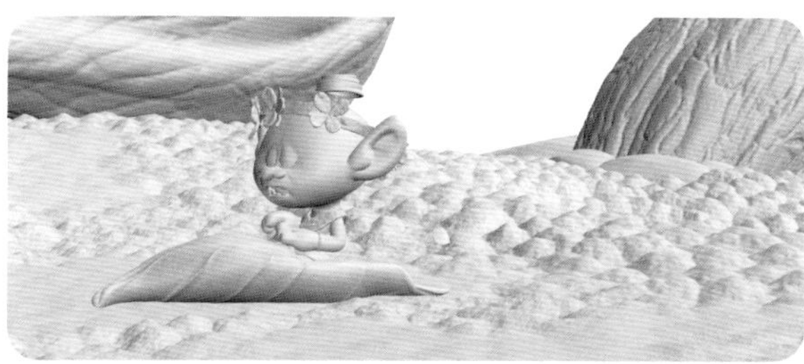

Technically, maintaining the fluorescent treatment throughout the sequence proved challenging for the surfacing team. "We wanted the characters to look brighter than the lighting conditions they were in," says Visual Effects Supervisor Philippe Denis. "It took us a few iterations in surfacing and lighting, but once we got a look in the ballpark of what we liked, we knew it would work. From there, it was just polishing the look to achieve our desired results."

Crafting that polished looked fell to the surfacing team, led by Head of Surfacing Lisa Slates Connors. "The sequence was unique due to the large number of custom creatures and singing plants," offers Connors. "The fact that they all had to become 'fluorescent'—that is, they had to glow—presented enormous challenges because, in some cases, the glow fades in or fades out."

Adding to the challenge was that most of the glowing creatures are fuzzy and many had to glow at the same time. Adds Connors, "We needed to add glowing shaders to the fuzz, the hair, and the skin underneath each creature. Consequently, the surfacing and lighting departments had to work together closely in order to achieve the desired effect."

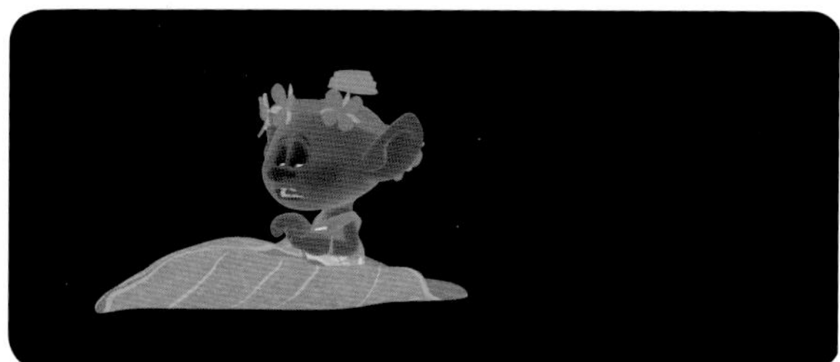

Below: Creature surfacing by Tsun-Hui Andrea Pun, tree surfacing by Paolo José deGuzman; *Right*: Poppy surfacing by Tsun-Hui Andrea Pun, environment surfacing by Carson James McKay

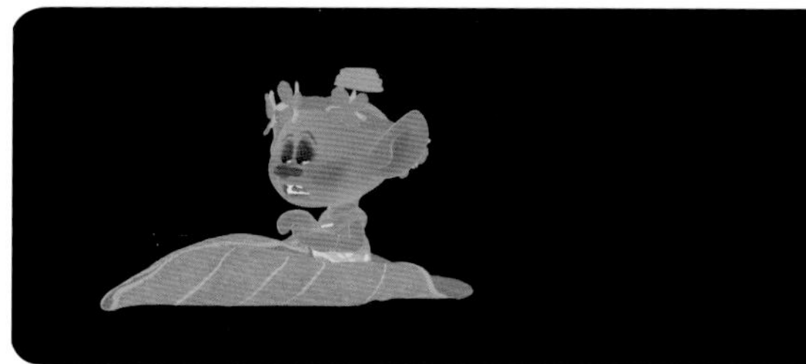

Animation

Top: Scott Lemmer; *Middle*: Drew Adams; *Bottom*: Mark Donald

For the animation team, led by David Burgess, the main challenge of Sequence 1100 was to explore Poppy and Branch's relationship in what is a very honest, very intimate moment for the characters. "There is a subtle battle of wills taking place as they are forced to get along," explains Supervising Animator Mark Donald. "It was challenging to have each reaction feel genuine in that moment and equally challenging to bring to life many of the forest critters and elements."

Both characters possess a strong visual style that the animators had to honor while also "keeping the animation fun, simple, and quirky," says Donald.

Before Poppy breaks into song, she and Branch argue, and in what is almost a throwaway beat, Poppy mimics Branch under her breath. The success of this subtle moment can be attributed to the animation. "We were initially unsure about the idea when I pitched it, mainly because we didn't want Poppy to come across as too annoying or sarcastic," explains Donald, "but I thought that this type of reaction would highlight how she felt about Branch's constant complaining. Keeping the idea subtle was super important because she was still very lonely and a little sad."

Effects

At the start of the sequence, the visual treatment is pretty minimalist. Despite the big forest behind Poppy and Branch, the story and camera stay focused on the two Trolls and the space that separates the characters, while the background elements remain purposely out of focus.

But once Poppy—the Troll who never gives up—decides to get back at Branch with a full-on number, everything changes. Explains Visual Effects Supervisor Philippe Denis, "The camera goes wider, the depth of field opens, a bunch of creatures become animated, and the light comes on stage like on a Broadway show."

In a few beats, the scene goes from a lonely, moonlit campsite to a fluorescent-lit set crowded with a multitude of characters.

"From a cinematographic perspective, the biggest challenge was to make the mood transformation seamless and totally believable for the audience," continues Denis. "The timing is important but all the details had to work together so nothing breaks the charm."

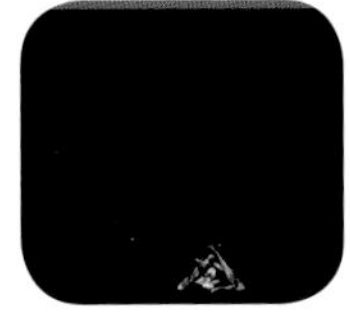
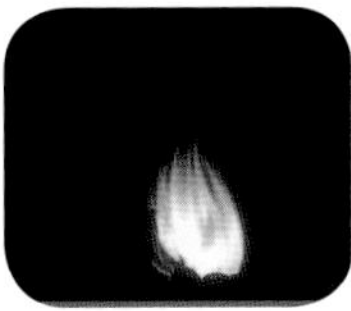

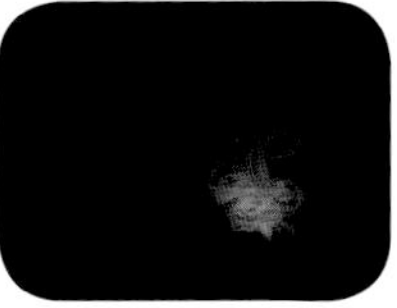
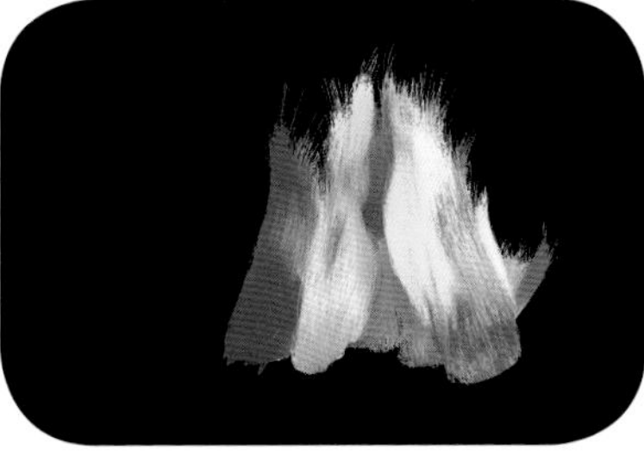

This page: Fire effects by Stephen Wood, smoke effects by Ashwin Prasad

Lighting

One of the most unusual aspects of the sequence is the atmosphere, which gives the impression that Poppy's performance takes place under a black light. Furthermore, this theatrical look emerges from a scene lit with natural light—just the moon and campfire provide the initial illumination.

To balance this transition, the lighting and surfacing departments had to work in tandem. "The creatures needed two separate looks," explains Digital Supervisor— Locations Mark Fattibene. "One look needed to fall in step with other characters and environmental elements, while the second look was their saturated fluorescent 'stage makeup.'"

Normally, it would be somewhat challenging for the lighting team to determine when to switch between two looks, but as Fattibene observes, "The music provided cues for us to follow, switching between looks to match the phrasing and cadence of the song."

Sequence 1100 proved to be one of the favorite scenes of the film among the crew. "This sequence is a perfect example of the inspiration that the crew gets from the story and how a tiny idea can snowball from artist to artist down the pipeline, where everyone is electrified and it shows up on screen," praises Producer Gina Shay.

As the scene ends, the creatures retreat into their hiding places and Poppy settles in the for night. "It's a great moment in the movie, as we now have a sense of where their relationship stands," observes Co-Producer Holly Edwards. "We're rooting for Poppy to break through to Branch as they press onward to Bergentown."

Left: Christy Page, Lighter; *Below*: Paul Hamler, Lead Lighter

Cloud Guy

Almost at their destination, Poppy and Branch reach a crossroads of sorts. As in the moment in *The Wizard of Oz* when Dorothy comes to an intersection in the Yellow Brick Road and the Scarecrow advises her which path to follow, the Trolls meet Cloud Guy, who helps them make their choice, although he's not as direct as the Scarecrow. Full of quirks, Cloud Guy quickly achieved cult status among the crew.

Bringing to life the character of Cloud Guy was Co-Director Walt Dohrn, who also provided the voices of Smidge and Fuzzbert. No stranger to voice acting, Dohrn received costar billing in *Shrek Forever After*, where he played the scene-stealing villain Rumpelstiltskin.

For his role as Cloud Guy, Dohrn worked alongside Anna Kendrick and Justin Timberlake during numerous recording sessions. "Everyone seems to love Cloud Guy," says Dohrn. "It was such a pleasure to provide his voice, but an even bigger surprise was to work with Anna and Justin, all of us in character!"

Cloud Guy reveals himself in a kind of sleight of hand as the camera pans across a forest with clouds in the distance. One cloud pops into the foreground, opens his eyes and mouth, and starts talking to Poppy and Branch. The environment was designed as a location that feels like it is in between Troll Village and Bergentown—it still is a felty forest but features the Bergen hues of avocado green, orange, and gold, along with some hints of civilization like an old boot, some litter, and a rubber tire thrown in.

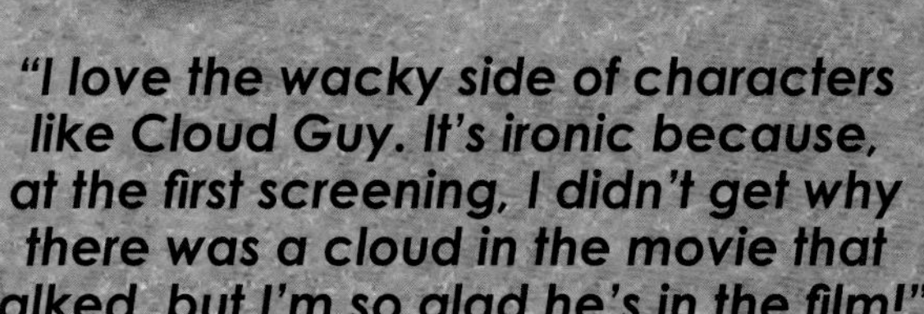

"I love the wacky side of characters like Cloud Guy. It's ironic because, at the first screening, I didn't get why there was a cloud in the movie that talked, but I'm so glad he's in the film!"

—Sandy Kao, Head of Rigging/Character Technical Director

Top: Cloud Guy Storyboards • Sean Charmatz; *Top right and right*: Cloud Guy Character Studies • Timothy Lamb; *Left*: Cloud Guy • Carlos Felipe León; *Bottom*: Cloud Guy Set • Priscilla Wong

TV STORE
LIQUIDATION
SPECIAL!
SALE!
SALE
PIZZA

TV
DONUTS
HOT
WELCOME TO
BERGENTOWN

Stark Suburbia

Previous pages: Bergentown • Alex Puvilland; *Below*: Bergen Living Room Sketch • Kendal Cronkhite-Shaindlin; *Bottom*: King's Chariot • Avner Geller

Where the Trolls are cute, kind, warm, fuzzy, and positive, the Bergens are their complete opposite: ugly, mean, cold, harsh, and negative. Make that *very* negative.

"The Bergens are very dour, angry, and sad. They don't connect with each other and they don't even look each other in the eye," says Director Mike Mitchell. Drawing a comparison that hits a little too close to home, he adds, "Much like we are with our smartphones, there is no connectivity between these creatures."

To create the look of the Bergens, the filmmakers again turned to Character Designer Craig Kellman. "When I was launched on the Bergens, I was told by the directors that they [the Bergens] were a large, evil race of Trolls who loved eating the little Trolls and were greedy capitalists to the Trolls' harmonious socialists," recalls Kellman.

From the perspective of the Trolls, the human-sized Bergens are enormous, towering figures that bumble around the forest. Despite this obvious size difference, the juxtaposition didn't factor into Kellman's process. "I took the size comparison into account when designing the Bergens, but the differences in scale didn't present any specific challenges for me," he explains. "I wanted them to have very different proportions than the Trolls so that the contrast was obvious and they weren't just scaled-up Trolls. They [the Bergens] have smaller heads in proportion to their bodies. The biggest difference between them physically in my opinion is how lumpy and grotesque they are compared with the cute streamlined shapes of the Trolls."

Although the Bergens remained "lumpy and grotesque," it was important to the filmmakers that the creatures come across as somewhat endearing and approachable. "We knew we did not want their skin to have the look or feel of a monster or lizard," explains Production

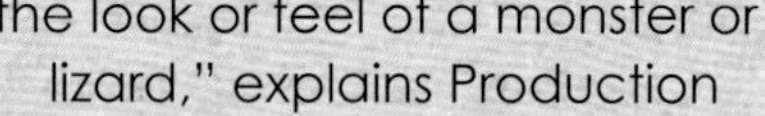

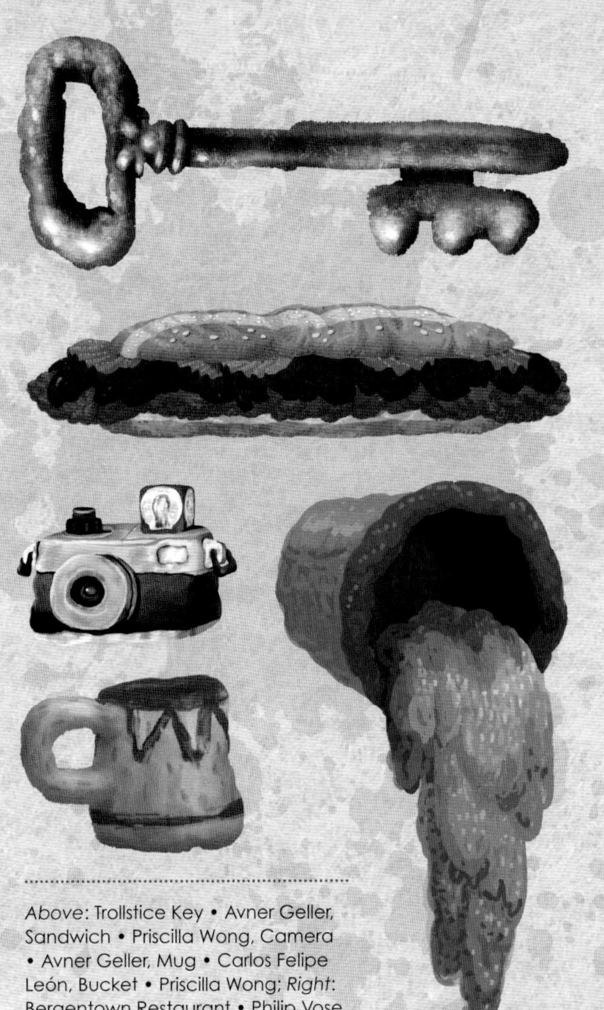

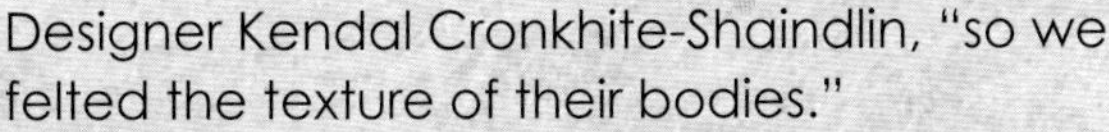

Above: Trollstice Key • Avner Geller, Sandwich • Priscilla Wong, Camera • Avner Geller, Mug • Carlos Felipe León, Bucket • Priscilla Wong; *Right*: Bergentown Restaurant • Philip Vose

Designer Kendal Cronkhite-Shaindlin, "so we felted the texture of their bodies."

The felted texture of the Bergens' skin also informed the animation department's process. "Initially, we wanted them to feel organic and fleshy," says Head of Character Animation David Burgess, "but the directors wanted them to feel like big stuffed animals, which allowed us a lot of freedom in our design and our approach to animation, resulting in a very distinctive look."

"Suburbanites" would be one way to describe the Bergens. More specifically, suburbanites from the era of disco, bell-bottom jeans, lava lamps, and Watergate. "I'm a child of the '70s," admits Cronkhite-Shaindlin. "[The Bergens] are suburbanites who live in houses, wear polyester, eat fast food, and, unfortunately, litter and pollute, just like in my childhood."

The palette chosen by Cronkhite-Shaindlin and her team includes multiple shades of avocado green, burnt orange, and an array of dull and shiny golds. "It is a combination of '70s sitcom and medieval storybook that pushes the extremes of both of those worlds," says Cronkhite-Shaindlin.

In direct contrast to the felted, fabric-inspired world of Troll Village and the forest, the world of the Bergens is based on real-world "human" textures: concrete, wood paneling, shag rugs, pavement, and Formica. New York School neo-expressionist renderings provided a huge source of inspiration for the crude shapes and textures. "Everything in Bergentown has a clay pinch-pot-like construction with bumpy surfaces," explains Cronkhite-Shaindlin. "That was our 'monster' visual shape language for the film, developed by Visual Development Artist Carlos Felipe León, who cracked this 3D code for us in the art department."

Because most of the film takes place in Bergentown, one of the biggest design challenges the filmmakers encountered was ballasting the miserable and unhappy nature of the Bergens so that it wouldn't overpower the story. "We had to have a layer of whimsy because we spend so much time there, and that's where the nostalgic color palette of the '70s comes in," explains Co-Director Walt Dohrn. "[Visual Development Artist] Philip Vose was the artist who launched us in this direction. With his combination of crude cartoon charm and '70s storybook design, he captured the look we wanted for Bergentown."

Bergentown

When Poppy and Branch finally arrive in Bergentown, it is very apparent that they are "not in Kansas anymore." A far cry from the vibrant palette of their home and forest, Bergentown resembles a depressing suburban interpretation of a medieval village.

The entire crew pored over numerous images of settlements from the Middle Ages, which influenced the general layout of the town. To deliver a sense of depth and perspective, the artists initially modeled Bergentown on walled European villages built on precipices.

The artists took this old foundation and then renovated it in a more contemporary style. "Bergentown pulls from the '70s, so the tackier, the better," says Production Designer Kendal Cronkhite-Shaindlin.

Continues Producer Gina Shay, "The stark and tacky white of the Castle provides a sharp contrast to the textures of the rest of the town, which is basically a combination of harsh metallic hues mixed with dark greens, oranges, and golds."

"Bergentown is the unhappiest place on Earth."
—Mike Mitchell, Director

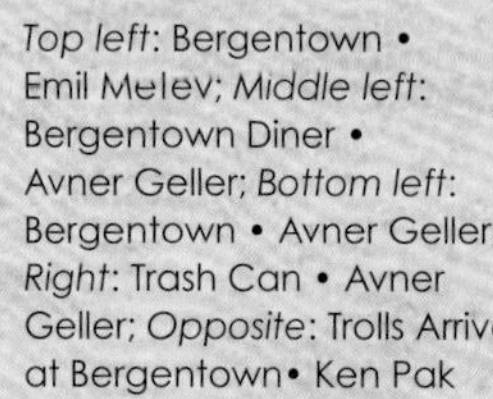

Top left: Bergentown • Emil Melev; *Middle left*: Bergentown Diner • Avner Geller; *Bottom left*: Bergentown • Avner Geller; *Right*: Trash Can • Avner Geller; *Opposite*: Trolls Arrive at Bergentown• Ken Pak

Opposite: Bergentown • Ken Pak; *Opposite, inset*: Troll Tree • Priscilla Wong; *This page*: Bergentown props • Avner Geller

BERGEN TOWN
PIZZA
PIZZA

Pizza
TV
EATS

Previous pages: Bergentown Establishing Shot • Ken Pak; *Top left*: Bergentown Street Lamps • Avner Geller; *Top right*: Water Tower • Sebastien Piquet; *Above*: Bergentown Establishing Shot • Ken Pak; *Opposite, top*: Gas Station • Avner Geller; *Opposite, bottom*: Laundromat • Avner Geller

GAS
SNACKS
13
CHANGE
25¢

Above left: Grabble Model • Sudipta Panja (initial model) and Paul Schoeni (final model); and Nar Nars Model • Anandha Sai (initial model) and Anand PG (final model); *Above middle:* Motel A Model • Anadha Sai (initial model) and Jaewon Lee (final model); *Above right:* Flurg Model • Anandha Sai (initial model) and Jaewon Lee (final model); and TV Shack Model • Amrut Raju Greptz and Amrut Raju; *Far left:* Bergentown Signs • Avner Geller; Below: Bergentown Buildings • Avner Geller; *Opposite, top:* Bergentown Buildings • Avner Geller; *Opposite, center:* Bergentown Signs • Avner Geller; *Opposite, bottom:* Bergentown Gate • Priscilla Wong

HAIR & DENTAL
GROOBS
2+1 Root CANALS
B'BLY'S BIBS
DONUTS
KING PLAZA/ DOWNTOWN
72X
BERGEN
Town

The Castle

According to Art Director/Character Designer Timothy Lamb, the whimsical, off-beat look of the royal Castle—the dominant architectural feature of Bergentown—was inspired by the abstract expressionism of certain artists from the New York School. "We loved the round and chaotic quality of some of their work and felt it was a great reference from which to design a castle and town built by monsters," says Lamb.

Along with Visual Development Artist Simon Rodgers, the two developed a shape language that was top-heavy so that the structure became, as Lamb puts it, "a castle so comically unstable that it looks imposing and ridiculous all at once."

Following the '70s references that guided much of the overall Bergen design, Lamb and Rodgers turned to kitschy architecture of the era such as the Madonna Inn in San Luis Obispo, California, and the Hollywood Castle for further inspiration. "Those buildings had the tacky '70s charm that we loved so much—something that remained at the core of our sense of humor while designing the castle and setting the tone for Bergentown," he says.

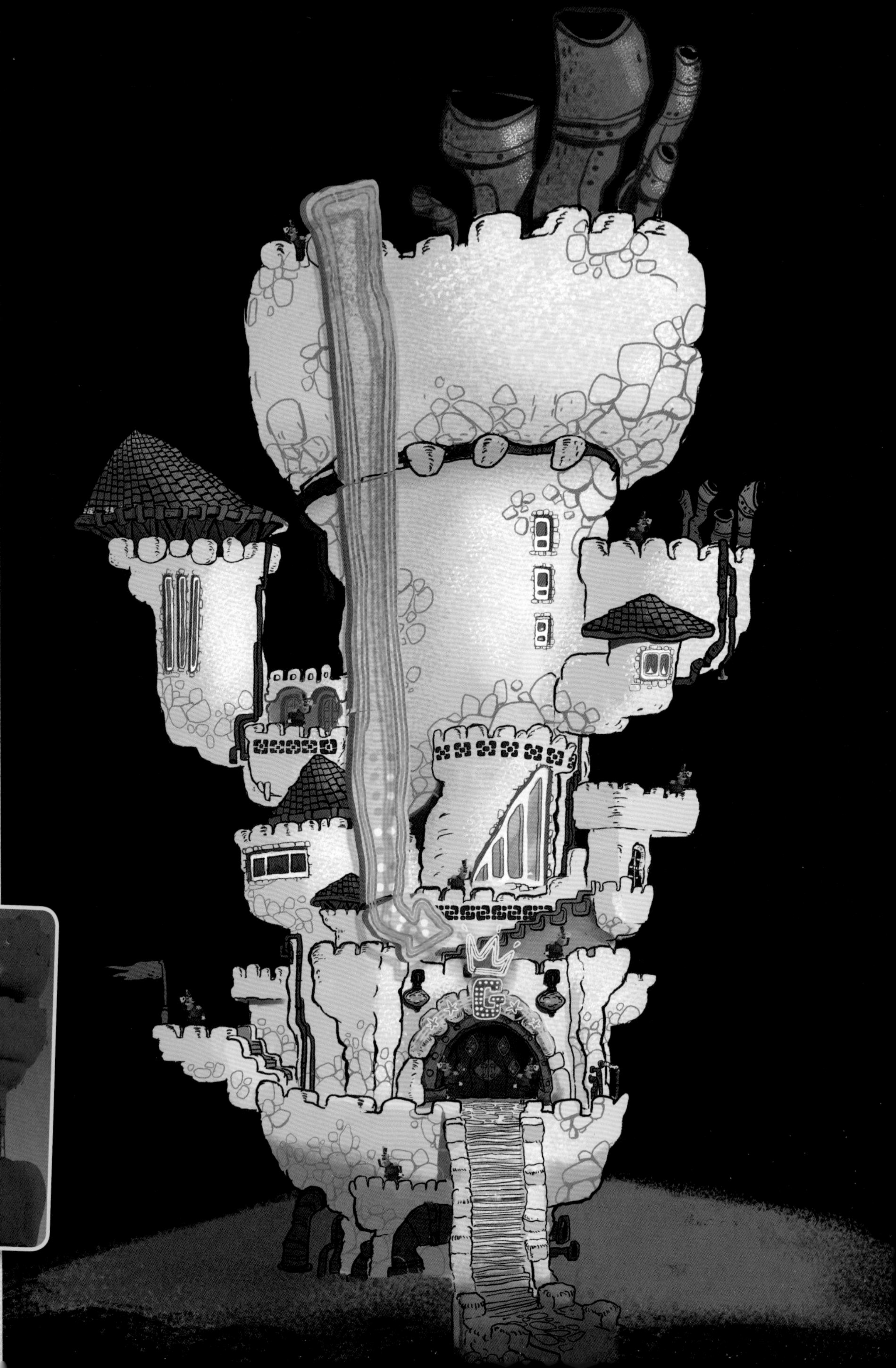

Above: Castle Exterior • Simon Rodgers; *Right*: Castle Details • Avner Geller

Below: Castle • Ritchie Sacilioc; *Top right:* Castle • Philip Vose; *Middle right:* Castle • Ritchie Sacilioc; *Bottom right:* Castle Set Design • Philippe Brochu

Left: Bergentown Exterior • Philip Vose; *Above*: Castle Wall Lamp • Kirsten Hensen Kawamura; *Opposite, top left*: Old King Table and Chairs • Kirsten Hensen Kawamura; *Opposite, top right*: Deer Painting • Kirsten Hensen Kawamura; *Below*: Castle Hallway • Richard Daskas

The Throne Room

The essence for this room, like all the interior spaces in the castle, was derived from a combination of '70s interior design mixed with medieval architecture. "For inspiration, we looked at the interiors of hotel lobbies from the '70s and combined that reference with castle banquet hall interiors to find that perfect balance," says Production Designer Kendal Cronkhite-Shaindlin.

Visual Development Artist Kirsten Hensen Kawamura poured over hundreds of photographs of '70s interiors to find the perfect combination of elements for the design of this set, which ultimately included a psychedelic shag carpet, hammered metal sculpted walls and ceilings, plastic plants in stone planters, and bubble glass windows.

Left: Throne Room Door • Kirsten Hensen Kawamura; *Above*: Creature heads • Kirsten Hensen Kawamura; *Below*: Throne Room Food • Kirsten Hensen Kawamura; *Bottom*: Dining Room • Kirsten Hensen Kawamura

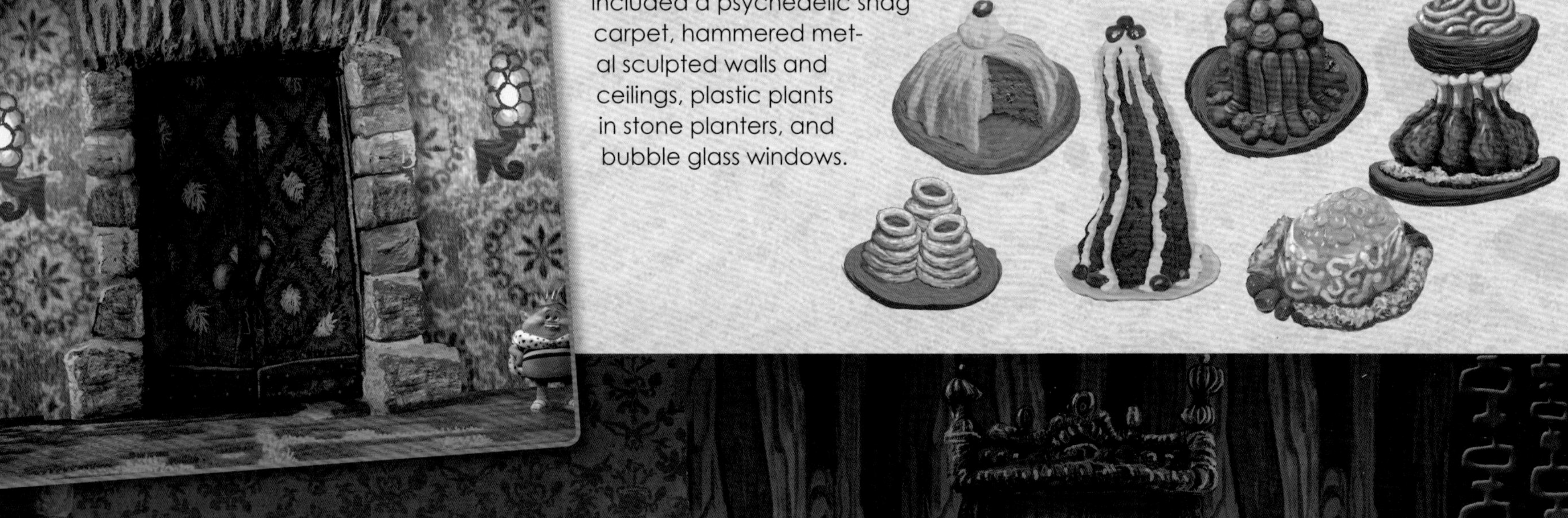

Left: King Gristle Banquet • Philip Vose; *Above*: Cage and Lock • Kirsten Hensen Kawamura; *Below*: Tableware, Normal Day • Kirsten Hensen Kawamura

The Kitchen

Described by the filmmakers as a "kitchen fit for an evil cooking show host," Chef's lair combines the '70s palette with a medieval monster vibe. The eclectic combination of appliances includes a cauldron that bubbles inside a fireplace, a '70s range, and a rather intimidating meat grinder. The food served at the Castle was inspired by 1970s "fad diet" recipe cards—jellied salads, sandwich cakes, and wiener roasts grace the King's table.

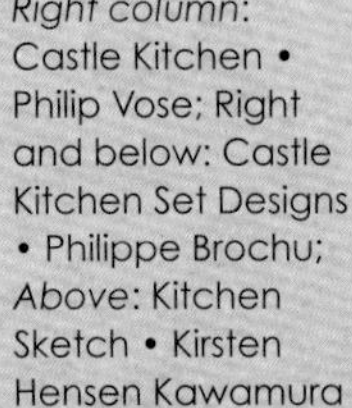

Right column: Castle Kitchen • Philip Vose; Right and below: Castle Kitchen Set Designs • Philippe Brochu; *Above*: Kitchen Sketch • Kirsten Hensen Kawamura

Above: Kitchen Tools • Kirsten Hensen Kawamura; *Below*: Kitchen Window Corner • Kirsten Hensen Kawamura

Bridget's Room

Poor scullery maid Bridget has no choice but to bring her work home with her. More specifically, the work just falls through a trap door onto the floor of the kitchen, which is directly over her room. The perpetual pile of dishes, pots, and pans never seems to get any smaller.

Tucked away in a corner of the room is Bridget's bed on a base of wooden crates and straw. Hanging on the walls of her little oasis are collage cutouts from her favorite magazine just like those you might expect to see in any teenage girl's room, including large, glamorous pictures of her idol and crush, King Gristle Jr.

Clockwise from top right: Sad Bridget • Carlos Felipe León; Bridget Washing • Carlos Felipe León; Bridget's Room • Sebastien Piquet; Hairbrush • Sebastien Piquet

Left and above: Bridget Props • Sebastien Piquet; *Below*: Bridget's Room • Ken Pak

Mr. Bibbly's

On the eve of his first Trollstice, King Gristle Jr. must make a very important pilgrimage to Mr. Bibbly's Bib store to purchase the perfect bib for eating Trolls.

Played by New Zealand comedian Rhys Darby, Bibbly is beside himself when a living being—let alone the king himself—enters his establishment for the first time in twenty years. Ever since the Trolls escaped Bergentown, there hasn't been a need for anyone to purchase one of his bibs.

Now, with Chef's promise to bring Trollstice back to the Bergens, Bibbly prepares for a surge in sales. No Bergen would think of showing up for Trollstice—a somewhat formal affair in Bergentown—without one of Mr. Bibbly's famous bibs.

Bibbly's is very refined for a Bergen and the design of his store reflects this. To give Mr. Bibbly's establishment the vibe of a high-end '70's boutique, Visual Development Artist Jayee Borcar populated his designs with white cabinetry, marbled mirrors, upholstered walls, and ostrich feathers.

"I'm the king who is bringing back Trollstice! I need a bib to match!"
—King Gristle Jr.

Left: Bib Props • Kirsten Hensen Kawamura; *Below*: Bib Fitting • Carlos Felipe León; *Bottom left*: Mr. Bibbly Character Study • Craig Kellman; *Bottom right*: Bib Corner • Jayee Borcar; *Opposite*: Bib Store • Philip Vose

Bibby's BIBS
BUY 10 BIBS FOR A FREE T.V.
PUOSE

Captain Starfunkle's

For his first date with Lady Glittersparkles, King Gristle Jr. pulls out all the stops and takes her to the town's most happening spot: Captain Starfunkle's Mini Golf Roller Rink and Arcade. "It's the go-to place if you're a Bergen," says Director Mike Mitchell.

Tucked away in a corner of the arcade is a pizza parlor, which provides the perfect backdrop for our star-crossed pair to share a romantic dinner. Bergens, according to the filmmakers, are partial to greasy pepperoni. "Naturally, our classic '70s inspiration was a romantic Shakey's-like pizza place, complete with red leather booths!" confesses Production Designer Kendal Cronkhite-Shaindlin.

Although never identified by name, the filmmakers unofficially affirm that the waiter who brings King Gristle Jr. and Lady Glittersparkles their pizza is none other than Captain Starfunkle himself (voiced by director Mike Mitchell).

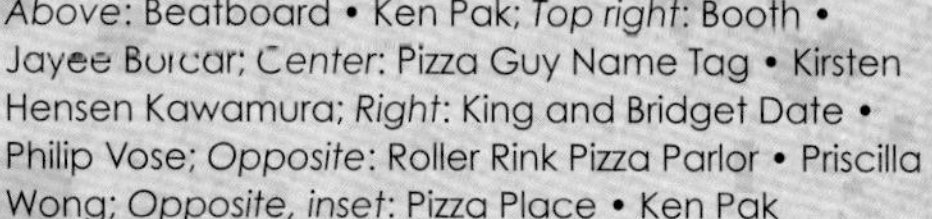

Above: Beatboard • Ken Pak; *Top right*: Booth • Jayee Borcar; *Center*: Pizza Guy Name Tag • Kirsten Hensen Kawamura; *Right*: King and Bridget Date • Philip Vose; *Opposite*: Roller Rink Pizza Parlor • Priscilla Wong; *Opposite, inset*: Pizza Place • Ken Pak

pizza
Capt. Starfunkles
SKATE
Mini-GOLF, ROLLER RINK & ARCADE
Pizza Skating
BIG FOOD
PIZZA

"We have been known more than once on this show to take the crew roller skating. There is a nostalgic '70's freedom feeling when cruising around the rink!"
—Gina Shay, Producer

Top: Pizza Ads • Jayee Borcar; *Above*: Pizza Date • Jayee Borcar; *Right*: Glittersparkles on Roller Skates • Claire Morrissey; *Far right*: Roller Skates • Kendal Cronkhite-Shaindlin; *Below*: Dance Machine • Danny Langston; *Bottom right*: Royal Skates • Carlos Felipe León

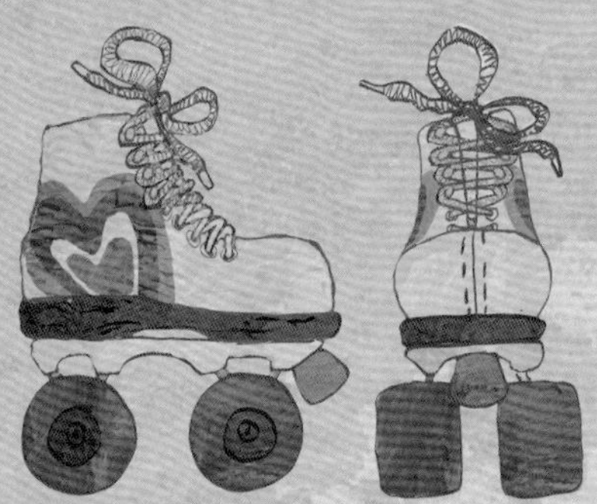

The roller-rink location also provides the launching pad for a fantasy sequence that takes the happy couple into orbit. As they skate against a backdrop of outer-space-themed designs, their world dissolves into a galaxy of planets and stars. "When you fall in love, it feels like you're flying through the universe, and that's what we wanted to convey with King Gristle Jr. and Lady Glittersparkles," says Co-Director Walt Dohrn.

Inspired in part by the roller rink located down the road from the DreamWorks Animation campus in Glendale, California, Cronkhite-Shaindlin designed King Gristle Jr.'s roller-rink fantasy set piece to perfectly capture the look of "the side of an airbrushed van from the '70s," according to Dohrn.

Recalling many a roller-skating party from the '70s, Mitchell adds, "Rest assured, we have that moment in the film when King Gristle Jr. and Lady Glittersparkles skate by the fan so they can cool off and, of course, let their hair blow in the wind—like we all did."

Above: Disco Ball • Jayee Borcar;
Left: Story Panels • Danny Langston;
Right: Roller Rink • Jayee Borcar;
Below: Color Key • Jayee Borcar

"Because Bridget's teeth stick out like picket fences, we did a lot experimenting to make sure that they didn't look like they were falling out when they moved."

—David Burgess, Head of Character Animation

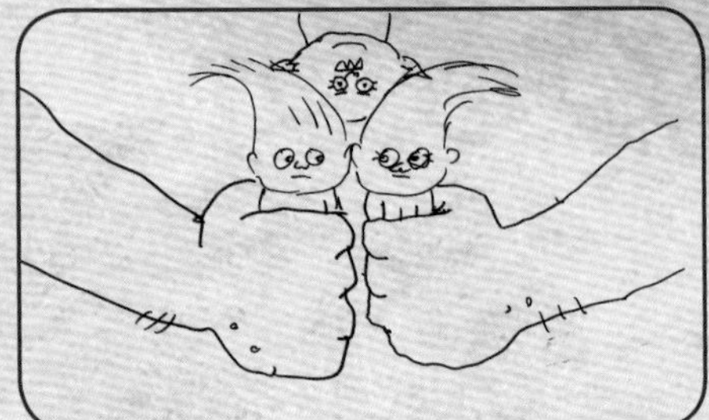

Opposite: Storyboards • Mike Mitchell; *Top Row*: Lighting Keys • Peter Zaslav and Avner Geller; *Above*: King Gristle Fantasy • Jayee Borcar; *Right*: King Gristle Fantasy • Peter Zaslav; *Below*: Fantasy Painting • Jayee Borcar

King Gristle Jr.

King Gristle Jr., the former Prince Gristle, is the obnoxious, petulant twenty-something king of the Bergen monsters. He inherited the crown at a young age when his father was forced to abdicate the throne by his disloyal subjects after he presided over the escape of the Trolls (a Bergen delicacy).

Mortified by his father's blunder and desperate to make his subjects love him, the younger Gristle vowed to put Trolls back on the menu and, in the process, bring happiness back to Bergentown.

Like all Bergens, King Gristle Jr. is, in a word, ugly. He was originally sketched by Director Mike Mitchell, but it was up to Character Designer Craig Kellman to turn the young king into a fully realized character. "He was pitched to me as a very spoiled, narcissistic little brat of a prince," recalls Kellman. "I liked that he would be really ugly but in love with himself, very confident, and that Bridget would see him as a dreamy heartthrob."

The spoiled royal is brought to life by Christopher Mintz-Plasse, who also voiced Fishlegs in the *How to Train Your Dragon* films.

Left: King Pose • Craig Kellman; *Right*: King Gristle Jr. Sketch • Mike Mitchell; *Below*: Early Bergen King Exploration • JJ Villard

This page: King Gristle Jr. Character Studies • Craig Kellman

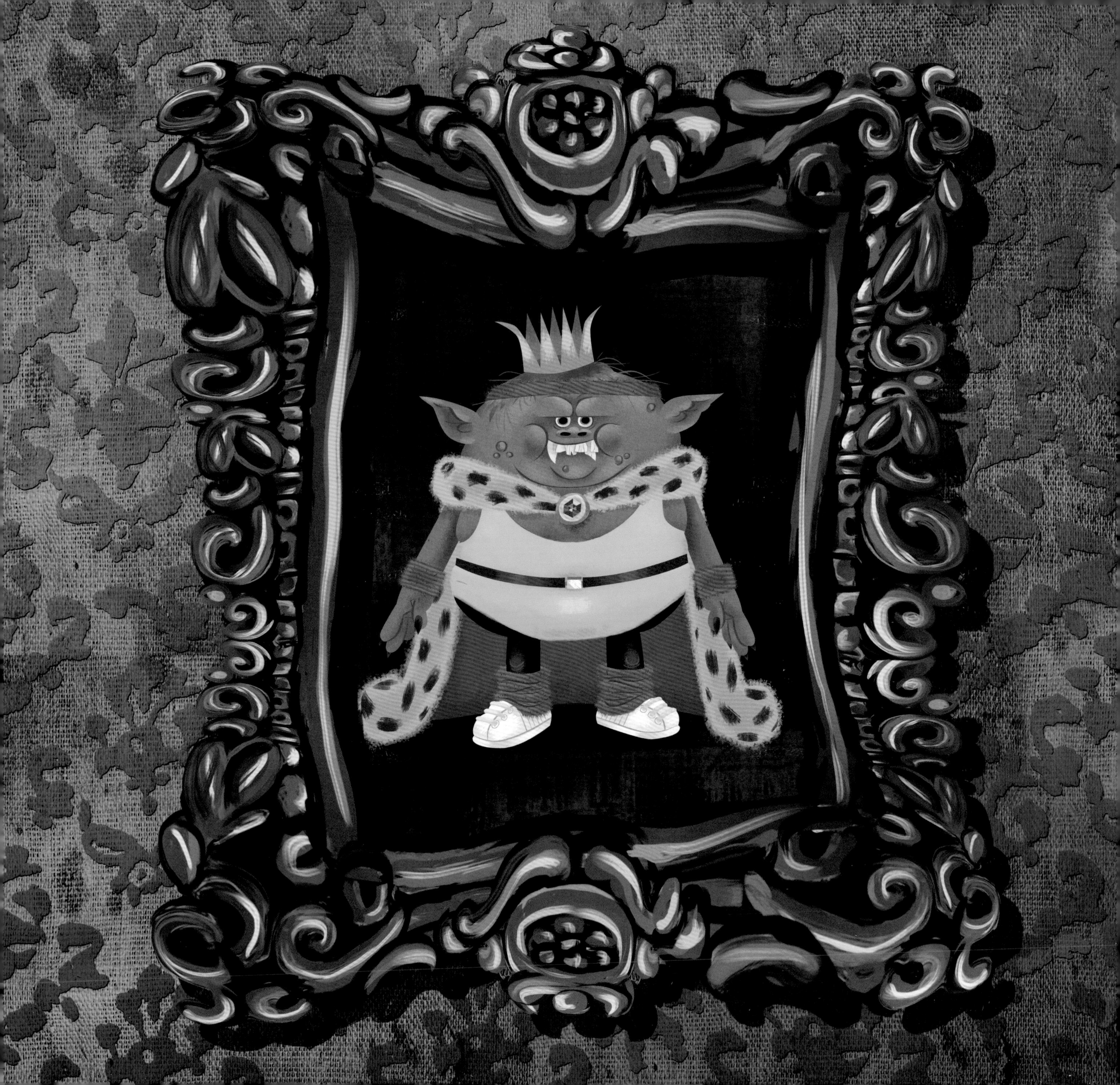

"He's that guy who still wears the same clothes he grew out of in high school."
—Walt Dohrn, Co-Director

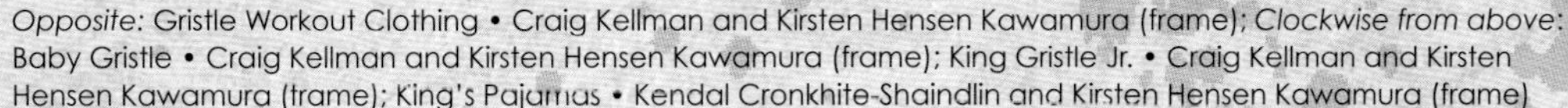

Opposite: Gristle Workout Clothing • Craig Kellman and Kirsten Hensen Kawamura (frame); *Clockwise from above:* Baby Gristle • Craig Kellman and Kirsten Hensen Kawamura (frame); King Gristle Jr. • Craig Kellman and Kirsten Hensen Kawamura (frame); King's Pajamas • Kendal Cronkhite-Shaindlin and Kirsten Hensen Kawamura (frame)

Left: Bergen Visual Development • Ken Pak; *Top*: King's Car • Philip Vose; *Above*: King's Banquet • Philip Vose; *Right*: King Gristle Jr. Final Character Render • DreamWorks Animation

Chef

Everything fell apart for Chef twenty years ago when the Trolls escaped (which also cost the elder King Gristle his crown). Prior to her fall from grace, Chef had it all: a sterling reputation, an adoring public, admirers, and a coveted spot in the Royal Kitchen. But everything she had built crumbled like a bad soufflé the day the Trolls escaped from the Troll Tree.

Exiled to the forest, Chef has spent the last two decades searching for the Trolls and plotting her return. As luck (hers) would have it, she stumbles upon Troll Village and is able to kidnap Poppy's best friends, the Snack Pack. Tucking them away in her fanny pack, she returns to Bergentown a hero, promising the ultimate gift to young King Gristle Jr.—his first taste of a Troll!

But like any great villain, Chef has ulterior motives. "Ultimately, she wants to be queen," explains Co-Director Walt Dohrn.

Ironically, Chef and Poppy have somewhat similar agendas. "Poppy just wants everyone to be happy," says Dohrn, "and Chef, in order for her evil plot to succeed, *needs* the Bergens to be happy."

Emmy Award winner Christine Baranski's vocal performance as the maniacal culinary artist is nothing short of delectable.

"Please give it up for your keeper of the Trolls . . . Your minister of happiness . . . Your royal chef: me!"
—Chef

Far left: Chef • Avner Geller; *Above left*: Chef Character Study • Craig Kellman; *Left*: Chef's Trailer Lighting Study • Rachel Tiep-Daniels

This page: Chef Character Studies • Craig Kellman

Top: Knives • Avner Geller; Above: Chef • Walt Dohrn; Right: Chef Villain Costume • Timothy Lamb; Below: Cleaver • Avner Geller

Below: Disheveled Chef • Craig Kellman, *Right*: Chef Final Character Render • DreamWorks Animation

Bridget

Every once in a while, a character comes along that is so endearing, so lovable, and so appealing, it leaves the audience wanting more and emerges as a breakout star. Such is the case with Bridget and her alter ego, Lady Glittersparkles. "Everyone on the crew has literally fallen in love with Bridget," gushes Producer Gina Shay. "Mike [Mitchell] and Walt [Dohrn] have truly created an amazing, memorable character."

"When we first came on board the project, we pitched an idea that centered around this character named Bridget and how the Trolls would help her," recalls Mitchell. "We basically started with this image of a monster-girl and there was something that just clicked."

As the put-upon scullery maid who lives beneath the Bergen king's castle, Bridget spends her days and nights at the beck and call of everyone in the royal palace, including King Gristle Jr., but she mainly serves her insufferable boss, Chef.

Unbeknownst to everyone, Bridget harbors a secret crush on young King Gristle Jr. To her, he's the dreamiest Bergen in the land. Of course, the king has no idea that Bridget is madly in love with him, nor is he even aware of her existence.

Although the directors clearly knew who Bridget was visually, it was three-time Golden Globe Award nominee Zooey Deschanel who brought the character to life. Working closely with the directors, Deschanel added her special perspective to Bridget's personality. "It was an exciting process," recalls Co-Director Walt Dohrn. "Zooey's voice is so distinctive and she added a layer of reality to Bridget."

Right: Bridget Character Study • Craig Kellman;
Far right: Bridget Sketch • Mike Mitchell

"Poppy and Bridget understand each other. Bridget is very sympathetic to the plight of the Trolls and is the only Bergen who befriends them."
—Kendal Cronkhite-Shaindlin, Production Designer

As recording sessions with Deschanel progressed, the directors worked with her to develop the primary features of Bridget's unmistakable voice. "It was Zooey who actually imagined Bridget as a combination of the timid shyness of Marilyn Monroe, the vulnerability of Cindy Brady, and a Valley Girl hanging out in a heavy-metal parking lot," recalls Dohrn. "It was brilliant."

To coax Bridget's timid and quiet side out of Deschanel, Director Mike Mitchell gave her the following advice: "Pretend that Bridget has a tiny little angel on the edge of her tongue and she doesn't want to wake it up!"

This page: Bridget Character Studies • Craig Kellman

"Bridget is a fun dichotomy—and a real departure visually from most characters in these types of movies."
—Craig Kellman, Character Designer

Above: Color Bridget Character Studies • Craig Kellman; *Right:* Bridget's Shrine • Ken Pak; *Opposite:* Bridget Final Character Render • DreamWorks Animation

Bridget's Fantasy

After each day of grueling work, Bridget pines away for King Gristle Jr. convinced that he has no idea she's even alive as she breaks into a rendition of Lionel Ritchie's "Hello." Her song turns into a love fantasy with life-size designs from her magazine cut outs—including paper-collaged tears. "When Zooey [Deschanel, as Bridget] sings Lionel Richie's 'Hello,' your heart breaks for her," confesses Co-Director Walt Dohrn.

Left column: Color Keys • Avner Geller; *Right column:* Fantasy Sequence • Kirsten Hensen Kawamura

Top left: Bridget Reading Magazine • Walt Dohrn; *Left and above*: Bergen Posters • Kirsten Hensen Kawamura

Lady Glittersparkles

As the story unfolds, Poppy and Branch end up in Bridget's room, where they find the Snack Pack held captive. Seeing Bridget, they assume that she's the culprit! But then the Trolls secretly watch Bridget sing Lionel Richie's "Hello" as she pines away for King Gristle Jr. "Poppy and all the other Trolls suddenly realize she actually has feelings," says Mitchell.

Knowing she cannot sit innocently on the sidelines, Poppy decides to make Bridget her own personal pet project. Letting her guard down, Poppy comes out of hiding and convinces Bridget that the Trolls will help her win over King Gristle Jr. in exchange for their freedom.

Taking the role of fairy godmother to a whole new level via a '70s makeover, Poppy and the Snack Pack transform Bridget into her alter ago, Lady Glittersparkles! Her transformation is nothing short of spectacular.

"They wanted Bridget to look like a '70s disco diva, with a jumpsuit and platform shoes, glittery makeup, and big rainbow hair," recalls Character Designer Craig Kellman. "The real credit for her design goes to Mike Mitchell. All I did was transcribe his direction and initial drawings using lots of great photo references from the '70s."

The crowning achievement of Poppy's efforts is Bridget's new wig, a cascade of color, glitter, and light. The wig is a weave of hair from Poppy and the Snack Pack that they style into a giant rainbow. One of the more complicated effects of the film, Bridget's rainbow wig comprises 237,375 strands.

Hiding inside the wig, the Trolls are able to whisper direction and offer advice to Bridget when she encounters King Gristle Jr. "The Trolls become Bridget's very own Cyrano de Bergerac," says Mitchell, "and they are the ones who give her the alias 'Lady Glittersparkles.'"

Without giving away a major spoiler in the film, suffice it to say Bridget realizes that it's not the glitter and glam on the outside that matters, but rather it's the stuff on the inside that counts.

Opposite: Lady Glittersparkles Final Character Render • DreamWorks Animation; *Top right*: Beatboard • Ken Pak; *Far right*: Lady Glittersparkles Character Study • Craig Kellman; *Right*: Lady Glittersparkles • Dave Smith

Coif Control

Below: Final Frame • DreamWorks Animation; Opposite, top and middle: Color Keys • Avner Geller; Opposite, bottom: Hair Storyboards • Sean Charmatz

Like any good hairstylist, Head of Character Effects Damon Riesberg knows his clients' coifs intimately. In this case, however, all his styling tools exist inside a computer, where it was entirely up to him to choreograph the movement and flow of the characters' locks.

"The [Troll dolls] were really our driving guide," says Riesberg. "We even did slow-motion reference footage so we could see how their hair reacted through a variety of motions."

To tame any potentially unruly locks, separate rigs were built for each character—one that allowed the character animators to control the body and one that gave the simulation artists the capacity to move the character's hair on its own. "Our more general rigs were built for overall motion and stability, whereas our simulation artists used controls with a much higher fidelity," explains Riesberg.

For Riesberg and the animation team, a few standout moments provided both technical and creative challenges. The first was "Poppy's Hair Stairs." In one of the more clever applications of hair, Poppy transforms her bright magenta mane into a glamorous staircase. These "Hair Stairs" had to look strong and sturdy and feature sharp angles while still conveying the warm fuzzy feeling so prevalent in Troll Village.

The second standout accomplishment was the design of Cooper's fur—a special variation on standard Troll hair that required almost twenty times more strands than the hair on a character's head. "We kept getting the note that Cooper's fur needed to feel 'light,' which is very subjective," recalls Riesberg. "We decided to take the essence of what we believed 'light' should look like and achieve that quality through motion."

Deciding to forgo initial models of the character in motion, the team looked to simulation properties and gauged "lightness" from that.

In addition to the ones Riesberg calls out, the crew also faced a number of other hair challenges. For instance, connecting Satin's and Chenille's hairs and animating them together as one unit was an enormous technical undertaking. Given the combined "hair count" of 117,920 strands between the twins, the effects team had to figure out how to make the hair move in sync so that it looked light and airy, rather than like a giant tube. To accomplish this, the filmmakers developed a special software program that combined specific hair follicles in the middle. "The connecting magic happens as a postprocess to the animation pipeline, but the animators have enough control to achieve the various poses and silhouettes required for each shot," explains Riesberg.

Finally, in what is sure to go down as one of the most memorable makeovers in film, Poppy and the Snack Pack (Biggie, Guy Diamond, Cooper, The Fashion Twins, DJ Suki, Smidge, and Fuzzbert) join forces to create a showstopping rainbow wig for Bridget. A cacophony of color and glitter, the wig contains 237,375 individual strands of hair—the most of any character other than Cooper.

Hair...
by the Numbers

CHARACTER	NUMBER OF STRANDS
Poppy (TOTAL)	83,705
Candlewick Hair Style	31,873
Pony Tail	51,832
Branch	49,861
Satin & Chenille	117,920
Guy Diamond	62,031
Creek	90,024
Cooper (TOTAL)	803,226
Hair	40,575
Fur	762,651
Smidge	57,535
Fuzzbert	117,997
Painter Troll	27,044
Bridget	120,558
Toddler Bridget	50,576
Lady Glittersparkles	237,375
TOTAL	1,817,852

"The Trolls are loved by so many generations. I remember friends having them when I was a kid in the 1970s. When you picked them up, you couldn't resist playing with their long colorful hair, twisting it between your fingers."

– Kendal Cronkhite-Shaindlin, Production Designer

King Gristle Sr.

Every leader aspires to leave a lasting legacy. Unfortunately, for King Gristle Sr., he will forever be remembered as the ruler in charge on the day the Trolls escaped from Bergentown. Once the most anticipated event of the year, Trollstice soon became a distant memory, leaving the citizens of Bergentown to live out their days with little to look forward to. "It's pretty grim for King Gristle," admits producer Gina Shay. "He goes from being the most celebrated king to the most loathed."

The voice behind the character riding this wave of emotions in none other than John Cleese, who, accordingly to Director Mike Mitchell, brings an "amazingly dry wit combined with pathos" to the character.

Designed by Character Designer Craig Kellman, King Gristle Sr.'s color scheme is a bit darker and more saturated than the ones used for the other Bergens, ensuring that he leaves a lasting impression during his brief appearance.

Above: King Gristle Sr. Portrait • Craig Kellman; *Top right*: Chandelier • Kirsten Hensen Kawamura; *Above right*: Fireplace • Kirsten Hensen Kawamura; *Below*: King's Bedroom • Kirsten Hensen Kawamura; *Opposite*: King Gristle Sr. Final Character Render • DreamWorks Animation

Bergens About Town

Following their general '70s inspirations for the Bergens, the filmmakers revisited iconic fashion of the era with its earth tones, synthetic fibers, and high-waisted bell-bottoms and polyester leisure suits to design all the Bergen "extras" encountered in Bergentown during the course of the film. "Craig Kellman exaggerated the Bergens' wardrobe by taking 'weird' to a whole new level with tight clothes and high waists," says Director Mike Mitchell.

This page: Bergen Character Studies • Craig Kellman; *Opposite*: Color Bergen Character Studies • Craig Kellman

I ♥
Bibs

These pages:
Bergen Character Studies • Craig Kellman

Bergen Creatures

In contrast to the whimsical and colorful menagerie of creatures that populates the forest surrounding Troll Village, Bergentown is filled with beasts that are semiserious and drab. "The creatures that populate Bergentown needed to reflect the characteristics of its citizens," explains Director Mike Mitchell. "In other words: angry, sad, and morose . . . and funny."

To make sure the creatures would fit in with the inhabitants of Bergentown, the filmmakers turned to Character Designer Craig Kellman. Recalls Art Director/Character Designer Timothy Lamb, "We asked Craig to come up with the types of animals we would see in Bergentown, and he came back with these amazing designs inspired by a combination of reptiles, insects, and amphibians, mixed with chickens."

Below: Crocroach • Craig Kellman; *Right*: Elephly • Craig Kellman

Above, right, and far right: Bergen Bug Sketches • Craig Kellman; *Below left and below right*: Toad Rooster • Craig Kellman; *Bottom right*: Toad Rooster Sketch • Mike Mitchell

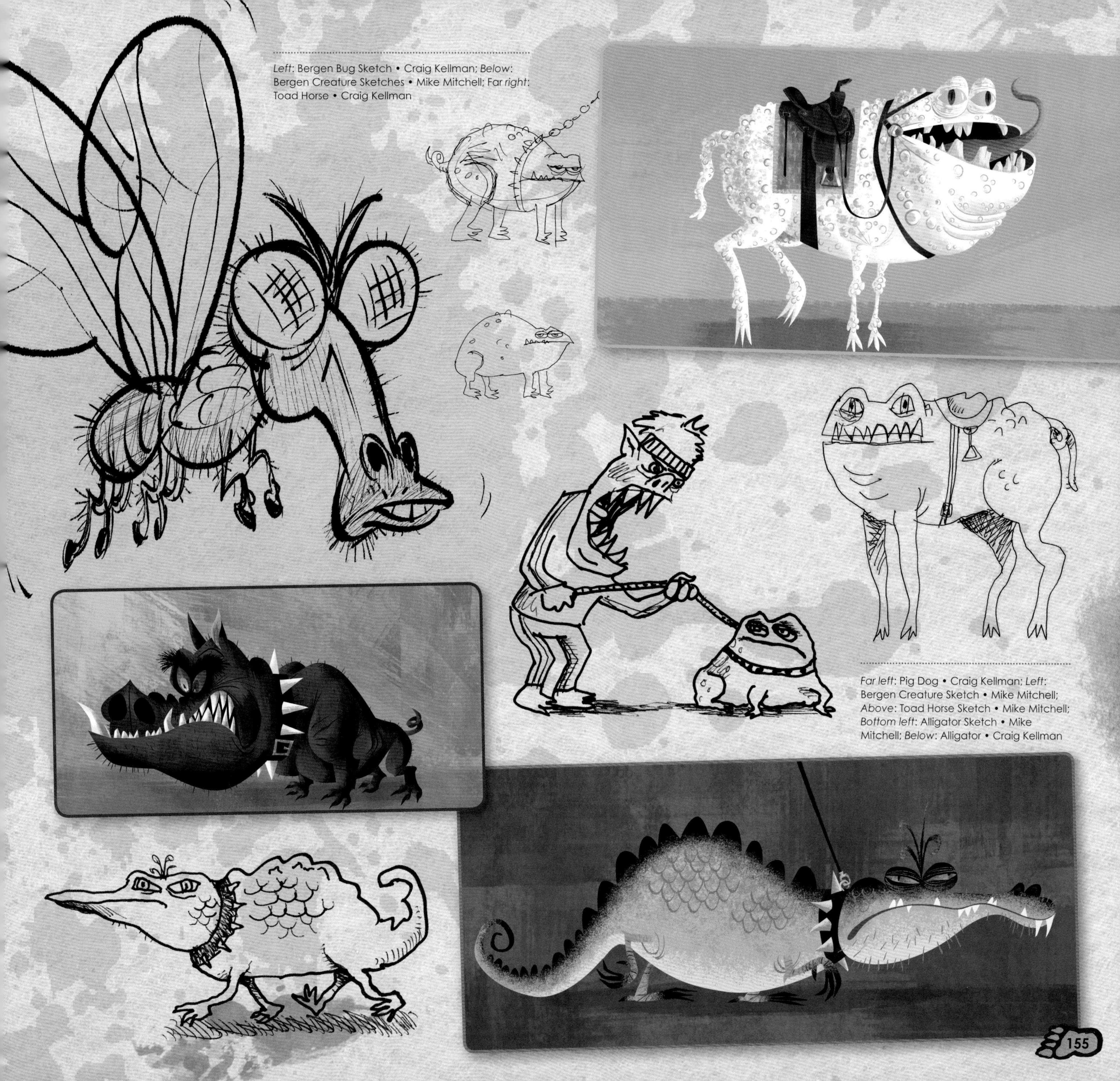

Left: Bergen Bug Sketch • Craig Kellman; *Below*: Bergen Creature Sketches • Mike Mitchell; Far *right*: Toad Horse • Craig Kellman

Far left: Pig Dog • Craig Kellman; *Left*: Bergen Creature Sketch • Mike Mitchell; *Above*: Toad Horse Sketch • Mike Mitchell; *Bottom left*: Alligator Sketch • Mike Mitchell; *Below*: Alligator • Craig Kellman

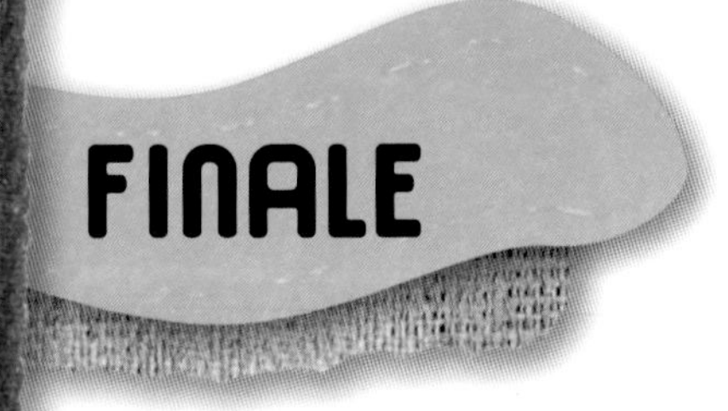

FINALE

Below: Branch and Poppy Final Character Renders • DreamWorks Animation • *Right*: Log Set • Sebastian Piquet

Mission accomplished: Branch is singing, the Bergens are singing, and everyone is happy beyond their wildest imaginations. For Poppy, this is a dream come true. Facing seemingly insurmountable obstacles, Poppy persevered.

"Poppy always knew that ultimately, she was responsible for her own happiness, and that starts from within," observes Director Mike Mitchell. "That's what this movie is really about: happiness comes from inside, so never give up."

Adds Producer Gina Shay, "For Branch, this journey provided a watershed moment. Knowing that he can let his guard down and the song in his heart out, he realizes that sometimes you just have to believe there is good in everyone and everything."

Like father like daughter, Poppy has proven to be a great leader, and is ready to usher in a new era for all—Trolls and Bergens alike. Long live Poppy, Queen of the Trolls!

"The story that Walt and Mike have crafted is so heartfelt. Poppy's interactions with Bridget and the ultimate realization by all the Bergens that happiness comes from within is such an emotional journey for both the characters and the audience. Watching the finale come to life on the screen is one my favorite moments in the film."

—Mireille Soria, Co-President, Feature Animation

Acknowledgments

Needless to say, it takes a village to create a book such as the one you just read. Thankfully, there was an amazing tribe of Trolls in the Village at DreamWorks Animation working on this project.

Below: DreamWorks Dedicated Unit Crew, Bangalore, India; *Far Right*: DreamWorks Animation Crew, Glendale, US; *Bottom*: Gifts • Avner Geller

A million thanks to Director Mike Mitchell, Co-Director Walt Dohrn, and Producer Gina Shay for their tireless support and hilarious interview sessions—it was an honor to work with you all again! Thanks to Jon Schmidt, Chiara Gillette, and Mallory Sparr for making the impossible possible when up against deadlines. Without the inspired work of Kendal Cronkhite-Shaindlin, Timothy Lamb, and every artist that worked on this film, we would be nowhere — so thank you all for your inspiration, talents, and undying love of all things groovy, weird, and psychedelic. Thanks of course to the marketing team at DreamWorks Animation: If I could appoint Debbie Luner "Queen of Bookland," I would, but for now, she'll have to settle for my undying gratitude. Thanks to Lisa Baldwin for her time and talents, and Jim Gallagher and Terry Curtin for their guidance and insights, and Casandra Tuttle for her eagle eye. At Cameron Books, thank you to Chris Gruener for the opportunity, Iain R. Morris for his amazing creativity and design work, and to Jake Gerli, editor extraordinaire! Finally, thank you to the indomitable Anna Kendrick for her contribution to this book. Anna: Your energy, passion, and talents are an inspiration to us all! —*Jerry Schmitz*

LA KINGS

Colophon

This page, below: Plant Swing • Chin Ko; *Endpapers*: Scrapbook Pages • Priscilla Wong, photographs by Samantha Trauben; *Front cover*: Forest Scene • Avner Geller; *Back cover, top left*: Beatboard • Ken Pak, *Top middle*: Disheveled Chef • Craig Kellman, *Top right*: King Gristle Jr. • Craig Kellman, *Bottom left*: Bridget's Room • Ken Pak, *Bottom right*: Lady Glittersparkles • Craig Kellman

PUBLISHER CHRIS GRUENER
CREATIVE DIRECTOR IAIN R. MORRIS
DESIGNER BARBARA GENETIN
EDITOR JAKE GERLI
MANAGING EDITOR JAN HUGHES
COPY EDITOR JUDITH DUNHAM

CAMERON + COMPANY would like to thank the following: Anna Kendrick, Mike Mitchell, Walt Dohrn, Gina Shay, Holly Edwards, Kendal Cronkhite-Shaindlin, Timothy Lamb, Jon Schmidt, Tucker Scott Alleborn, Ian McIntosh, Alex Weiss Morgan, Rafe Blood, Debbie Luner, Jim Gallagher, Lisa Baldwin, Sarah Maines, Bonnie Arnold, Mireille Soria, Adria Munnerlyn, Michael Garcia.

Academy Award nominee Anna Kendrick has a variety of accomplishments that showcase her impressive range of talent. She was the lead in *Pitch Perfect 2*, which broke the record as the highest grossing musical of all time, and the song "Cups," which she performed in the first *Pitch Perfect*, went multi-platinum.

Kendrick's other film credits include *Into the Woods*, *The Last Five Years*, *Cake*, *Happy Christmas*, *Drinking Buddies*, *50/50*, *End of Watch*, *Camp*, and *Up in the Air*, for which she earned Oscar, Golden Globe, Screen Actors Guild , BAFTA and Critics' Choice Award nominations. She also appeared in the first three installments of the blockbuster *Twilight Saga* franchise.

An accomplished theater veteran, Kendrick, at the age of 12, became the second-youngest Tony Award nominee in history, having received a nomination for Best Featured Actress in a Musical for her role as Dinah Lord in the 1997 Broadway musical production of *High Society*.

Self-professed pop-culture geek and sci-fi nerd, Jerry Schmitz most recently wrote *The Art and Making of the Peanuts Movie* and is the author of *The Art of Shrek Forever After* and *Surf's Up: The Art and Making of a True Story*, by Cody Maverick (spoiler alert: a penguin did not really write that book). He also keeps busy working in the film business as a marketing, publicity, and production consultant. If he were a Troll, he would be "Chocolatier Troll" (with his own shoppe). Follow him @ JerSchmitz.